579/66

Reading Style

Reading Style
A Life in Sentences

Jenny Davidson

Columbia University Press
New York

Columbia University Press
Publishers Since 1893
New York   Chichester, West Sussex
cup.columbia.edu

Library of Congress Cataloging-in-Publication Data
Davidson, Jenny.
Reading style : a life in sentences / Jenny Davidson.
    pages   cm
Includes bibliographical references and index.
ISBN 978-0-231-16858-8 (cloth : alk. paper) — ISBN 978-0-231-53740-7
(electronic)
1. Readability (Literary style) 2. Style, Literary. 3. Grammar, Comparative
and general—Sentences. 4. Grammar, Comparative and general—Syntax
5. Criticism, Textual. 6. Literature—Study and teaching. I. Title.

PN204.D38   2014
809—dc23   2013030998

Columbia University Press books are printed on permanent and durable
acid-free paper.

This book is printed on paper with recycled content.
Printed in the United States of America

c 10 9 8 7 6 5 4 3 2 1 .

Cover design by Julia Kushnirsky
Cover illustration by Mara Cerri

References to websites (URLs) were accurate at the time of writing.
Neither the author nor Columbia University Press is responsible for URLs
that may have expired or changed since the manuscript was prepared.

For my teachers,
my students
and
everyone else
who has ever talked
with me
about books

To snare a sensibility in words, especially one that is alive and powerful, one must be tentative and nimble. The form of jottings, rather than an essay (with its claim to a linear, consecutive argument), seemed more appropriate for getting down something of this particular fugitive sensibility.

—Susan Sontag, "Notes on 'Camp'" (1964)

The most direct probe of the intensity of our ludic readers' needs to escape from unpleasant consciousness is Question 3a in the Reading Habits Questionnaire (scored in chapter 5 as part of the Frustration Index); namely, how would one feel to discover, alone in a strange hotel, that one had nothing to read. This question elicited a range of replies from the 129 students readily scored in terms of their affective tone and intensity. These dimensions are even more clearly discerned in the response of the 28 ludic readers who replied to this question. In approximate sequence of intensity, with headings selected on intuitive grounds to describe the tone of the response, these 28 replies are set out below (if more than one reader made a given response the number who did so is indicated in parenthesis):

No emotion: nothing
Displeasure: restless (2), frustrated (5), annoyed, peeved, a bit hassled
Anger: bloody annoyed
Agitated: manic, bothered, a little upset, let down, disappointed, bad, bitterly disappointed, terrible
Anxiety: lost (2), quite lost, lost and miserable, really miserable, desolate!, awful/dispossessed, desperate

—Victor Nell, *Lost in a Book: The Psychology of Reading for Pleasure* (1988)

CONTENTS

Reading Style

1

The Glimmer Factor

Anthony Burgess's 99 *Novels*

I've always been bothered by the notion that literature is worth reading chiefly for what it teaches us about life. Of course we learn things about life from literature: it's self-evident that a book may make its reader wiser or more philosophical in some measure consequent upon the nature of the book itself, the timing and circumstances of the reader's encounter with it and the reader's openness to transformation. But there is also something intolerably banal about the idea that the main reward of reading a novel by Leo Tolstoy or George Eliot should be my becoming a slightly better person. Partly I am troubled that the motive of pleasure recedes so far from view. This kind of emphasis on self-improvement also steals the limelight from a more stringently cognitive aspect of reading. Not the simple fact of transportation, of being lost in a book,

but rather a form of intellectual play that seems to me ulti-
mately as ethical as its lesson-driven counterpart: ethical in
the sense of its developing one's capacities of comprehension
to the fullest, taking the jumbled furniture of the human mind
(the meager apparatus of Lear's "poor, bare, forked animal")
and teaching it to make meaning out of words. To make the
idea that literature tells us about life the primary reason for
reading Laurence Sterne, Jane Austen, Virginia Woolf and
their like degrades the very thing that draws me to literature
in the first place: the glimmer of the sentences, not first and
foremost the wisdom contained in them. By stripping literary
language down to its constituent parts, I perversely gain a
sense of transcendence, an emotional as well as intellectual
liberation that comes by way of the most precise consideration of details of language.

All sentences are not created equal. Some are more interest-
ing, more intricate, more attractive or repellent than others.
This book originated in a series of lectures I gave at Columbia
University in the fall of 2009. The course was called "On
Style," and we read through what I think of as one of the
central genealogies of the European realist novel (*Emma*,
Madame Bovary, *The Golden Bowl* and the opening chunk
of *In Search of Lost Time*) along with a more idiosyncratic
set of sequels in style: shorter pieces by Georges Perec, Roland
Barthes, Susan Sontag, Wayne Koestenbaum, Luc Sante and
Gary Lutz, and then W. G. Sebald's *The Rings of Saturn* and
Alan Hollinghurst's *The Line of Beauty*, with Sebald representing the culmination of one line of thought as to what
might be done in the novel by way of a Proustian first-person
subjective narrating intelligence and Hollinghurst standing for
the radical reimagining of a third-person mode of narration
associated with Gustave Flaubert and Henry James. That
sequence of readings remains the core of the book, though I
have trimmed the discussions of Flaubert and Marcel Proust

and permitted myself to roam more freely and waywardly between texts and topics than the license of a class syllabus necessarily permits. Most of all, I have allowed my extra-curricular reading to inflect the book's observations about style and sensibility. I am in possession of a novel-reading habit that invites terms like *compulsion* or *addiction*, and that on the face of things has little to do with my working life as a professor of literature. (Being a fast and voracious reader is not a necessity for academic life, merely a valuable convenience.) Visiting our family in the United States the sum-mer I turned five, my English grandmother was sufficiently worried about the extent and intensity of my reading that she wanted my mother to take me to the doctor, and my reading undoubtedly remains excessive, unbalanced.

My guide, in terms of the selection of texts, has been per-sonal taste, not representative coverage of the full range of possibilities for literary language in English. One reader of an earlier draft of this book commented on its having been fairly standard, in the middle of the twentieth century, to tell a story about the great tradition of fictional prose style that began with Austen or Flaubert, proceeded through James and Proust to high modernism (James Joyce, D. H. Lawrence, Woolf) and thence to Samuel Beckett or the French new novel (Alain Robbe-Grillet, Nathalie Sarraute et al.). To some extent I take that story for granted, but it's not a story I see the need to retell. Indeed, I am not really interested in mak-ing an argument about style, what it is and its genealogies in the Anglo-American novel. The rationale for the inclusion of each passage I write about is often just that it speaks to me strongly—that it has a high glimmer factor—or that it lets me single out some aspect of style on which I wish to comment. If there is an argument here, it operates in the fashion of a field notebook, by way of selection and description, as an entomol-ogist or ornithologist might not merely transmit something of a way of looking, sharpening the tools of perception, but perhaps also begin to elicit a deeper comprehension of how to know which objects most reward such scrutiny.

Francis Spufford called his memoir of childhood reading *The Child That Books Built*, and like Spufford, I feel that I have been largely shaped by the books I have read. I was a "word child," as one of Iris Murdoch's novels has it: novels were a means of escape, of transport from the quotidian (childhood is full of long boring stretches!), first into worlds like Narnia or Laura Ingalls Wilder's prairie but later into spaces less physically rendered and more purely conjured as constructions of language and intellect, T. S. Eliot's Waste Land, say, or Fyodor Dostoevsky's Grand Inquisitor's cell. As a precocious reader in late childhood and adolescence, one is forced to find intellectual guides in odd places: Robert Graves was an important one, leading me by way of *I, Claudius* to *The White Goddess* and from there to Sir James George Fraser's *The Golden Bough*, Robert Burton's *Anatomy of Melancholy* and Sir Thomas Browne's *Religio Medici*; the detective novels of Dorothy L. Sayers and Nicholas Blake sent me to Jacobean revenge tragedies and the pastiche work of Thomas Lovell Beddoes and A. E. Housman, and Ezra Pound's anthologies and works of criticism (especially *Confucius to Cummings* and *The ABCs of Reading*) opened up a route to Chapman's Homer and Hardy's lyrics. I cannot reread John Fowles in adulthood without my enjoyment of the novels being overshadowed by a sense of the unpleasant personality revealed by the posthumous publication of his journals, but *The Magus* and *The French Lieutenant's Woman* opened up worlds for me then. Perhaps my most indispensable guide was Anthony Burgess: the verbal playfulness of his Enderby novels in the first instance, but also the sub-Joycean byplay of his Shakespeare novel *Nothing Like the Sun* (in which Burgess voluntarily restricted his vocabulary to words Shakespeare could feasibly have known, allowing only a single exception, *spurgeoning*, a verb he coined to honor the critic Caroline Spurgeon), the intense linguistic inventiveness of *A Clockwork Orange*, the sparky polemical engagements of books like *The Wanting Seed* and *The End of the World News*.

And then I obtained a copy of Burgess's little guide 99 *Novels: The Best in English Since 1939*, and I was transfixed. It is a peculiar and cranky book, one that prompts the suspicion of its having been slapped together in considerable haste (in an interview, Burgess once claimed it had been written in two weeks). Novels are presented in chronological order, two or three for each year, perhaps contributing to some of the peculiarities of the selection (things like the omission of *A House for Mr. Biswas* or the inclusion of Norman Mailer's *Ancient Evenings*, which is pretty certainly *not* one of the best novels written in English since 1939). This slender volume, though, led me to *Pale Fire* and *Giles Goat-Boy* and *The Alexandria Quartet* and *At Swim-Two-Birds*, to Alasdair Gray's peculiar and brilliant *Lanark* (aside from its other distinctions, one of the great literary representations of skin disease) and V. S. Naipaul's dreadfully bleak *A Bend in the River*. One of the most significant reading experiences I had as a consequence of 99 *Novels* was *Gravity's Rainbow*, which I am not sure I would have persisted with otherwise at age fifteen, but which Burgess's praise persuaded me to make my way through with the help of a dictionary. One of the most striking features of Thomas Pynchon's style in this book is the crashing together of a number of different specialized vocabularies, a unique mélange that can be effectively evoked by synecdoche (*smegma, Ouspenskian, Poisson distribution*); it transformed my sense of what could be done in language.

I was lucky to be a student at an excellent independent school in Philadelphia—Germantown Friends School—that was also attached to a library that transcended the limitations of the ordinary school library, the Friends Free Library of Germantown. I worked there during summers in high school, and its small but excellent adult fiction collection, tucked away on an upstairs balcony, served almost as my private preserve during those years; the children's room at the Friends Free saw much heavier use, while adult readers of popular fiction would have sought out the much larger, more up-to-date and reader-friendly collection a few blocks away at the large public library branch on Chelten Avenue. The Friends Free held many of the books Burgess recommended—it was that sort of collection, high-middlebrow with not much to recommend itself to a reader less bent on self-education and mind expansion than my teenage self. That was where I found *Gravity's Rainbow* and the novels of Muriel Spark, Joyce Carol Oates and Doris Lessing, indeed of Burgess himself. I have a vivid memory of sitting at age thirteen in my polyester kilt and polo shirt on the bleachers at a Friday afternoon lacrosse game, immersed in Burgess's *Earthly Powers* ("It was the afternoon of my eighty-first birthday, and I was in bed with my catamite when Ali announced that the archbishop had come to see me") and very much hoping that the coach wouldn't puncture my readerly bubble by subbing me in. I was a terrible lacrosse player, but I liked the arcane names for the defensive positions I usually played, point and cover point; it speaks to the extent of my literary preoccupations that I often accidentally misremembered the second as "counter point," as in the Aldous Huxley title *Point Counter Point* (Huxley, according to Burgess's somewhat unbalanced account, having written three of the best ninety-nine novels published in English since 1939).

In the meantime I was also reading and rereading Austen, Charles Dickens, Anthony Trollope, *The Hobbit* and the Lord of the Rings trilogy, Josephine Tey, Alice Walker, Diana Wynne Jones, the stories of Arthur Conan Doyle and Robert Louis Stevenson: really, whatever came to hand. I experienced a shock of recognition when I came across a passage, quoted in Stephen Burt's biography of Randall Jarrell, in which Jarrell describes his own childhood: "A shrew or a hummingbird eats half its weight in twenty-four hours; when I was a boy I read half my weight in a week. I went to school, played, did the things the grown-ups made me do; but no matter how little time I had left, there were never books enough to fill it—I lived on the ragged edge of having nothing to read."[1] I read greedily, omnivorously and much too quickly for my own comfort: *The Tin Drum* and *Terra Nostra* were usefully copious fodder, and so were Anne McCaffrey's Pern novels and the complete works of Piers Anthony, Michael Crichton, Anne Rice, Robert Ludlum and a host of others.

Going to university and gaining firsthand access to one of the world's great research libraries would open up new dimensions of reading to me. I had hungered illicitly as a high school student for Barthes and Jacques Derrida, whose names were mentioned in the Sunday supplements but whose writings I would not have known how to get hold of. I remember with a tinge of remorse (it was certainly neither the first nor the last time I spent the night at a friend's house lost in a book) plucking *S/Z* from a shelf in my friend S.'s bedroom the summer after our high school graduation; her stepmother, to whom the book belonged, had done graduate work in literature, and Barthes's approach to literary analysis held for me the force of revelation. Now I immersed myself in the writings not just of Barthes and Derrida but of Gilles Deleuze and Félix Guattari, Gérard Genette, Victor Shklovskii and many others. A few years later, in graduate school, I would become a serious reader of John Locke and David Hume and Adam Smith and Edmund Burke and William Hazlitt. I have always had a particular soft spot for the novelist-essayists, writers like George Orwell and Rebecca West and James Baldwin whose genius resides more in the texture of thought in the prose than in one particular individual novel, but I would also increasingly encounter works of scholarship that possessed the near-magical force and clarity of my favorite novels: Erving Goffman's *The Presentation of Self in Everyday Life*, Derek Parfit's *Reasons and Persons*, Thomas Nagel's *Mortal Questions*, John Passmore's *The Perfectibility of Man*. Novels no longer had to serve as my proxy for the whole world of ideas.

The immersive reading of my childhood was a great gift, that ability to transport myself by losing myself in a book; so was the wide and deep exploratory reading of adolescence, with Burgess and others as my guide, and then the more intellectually focused reading I began to do at age seventeen or eighteen. But all along, from earliest childhood, I was practicing and honing a set of reading skills that would become not just a valuable professional or personal asset, a mode at once of consolation and of academic self-advancement, but actually my chief way of being in the world. This reading, it would not be hyperbolic to say, is what makes life itself worthwhile: there are other things I like to do also (running, swimming, yoga, eating cake), but I think I would die if I didn't have reading to protect me from the buzz of unwanted thoughts, the tedium of everyday existence, the stresses and strains of human interaction, etc. etc. This mode of reading has something in common, as I have already suggested, with the natural historian's way of looking closely and lovingly at things, of describing in order to understand, an orientation I associate especially with writers like Oliver Sacks or the British paleontologist Richard Fortey. It involves the application of a critical intelligence, more neutrally observing than judging or summing up and yet very ready to make selections and discriminations when they are called for. This kind of reading has been as much a compulsion for me as the more purely escapist forms of novel-reading to which I remain in thrall. Looking very closely at the style and techniques of certain literary works, books that will repay near-infinite amounts of reading and rereading, seems to me at once perversely unworldly and profoundly practical, at one and the same time supremely playful and deadly in earnest. It is what I spend a great deal of my time doing in the classroom: it may be valuable to arrive at broad thematic generalizations about a work or an author, but it strikes me as rash to try to answer the big questions about what something means if you can't yet parse the meanings of the words in one dense enigmatic sentence.

Reading Style is not my own 99 *Novels*. It has less to say about which books must be read than about how to read. That said, the book does offer a sort of anthology of prose styles, the primary logic for inclusion being strong personal preference rather than representative selection. In that sense, it's not a genealogy or taxonomy so much as it is a sampler of sentences I have loved. (Beckett is a notable omission, perhaps because I love his plays much more passionately than his prose fiction; play texts are outside the scope of this book, although I have long had a yen to write a little book on the history from earliest times to the present day of the stage direction, which seems to me to bear an interesting relationship to the forms of notation novelists would come to develop for representing human movement in third-person narration.)

The unit of taste in this case is the sentence, sometimes the paragraph, its structure and sensibility, its fugitive feel on the tongue. I strongly experience the allure of a certain type of box of chocolates not so much because of the chocolates themselves as because of the exquisite nature of the choice offered in map or legend. In my mother's family, that paper guide was known as a "suggester": a chart of sorts representing each chocolate's exterior and signaling (graphically, verbally) the delights contained therein. If I were choosing a box of Jacques Torres chocolates for someone else, I would pick the dark-chocolate selection because of its clear gastronomical superiority, but if I were buying it just for myself, a decadent and unlikely prospect, I would choose milk chocolate; dark chocolate may be aesthetically preferable to milk, but I like it much less than its sweeter, less pungent counterpart. My taste in prose differs from my taste in chocolate, but it similarly lacks a sense of proportion ("Truth is disputable, taste is not"). I love anchovies, I hate dill, but it would be absurd to construe my preferences as objective verdicts on the respective merits of those two foodstuffs. When I loathe a book, though, my passionate contempt is colored partly by my conviction that it's morally as well as aesthetically pernicious. I feel furious or even outraged by, say, the sentimentality of Markus Zusak's young-adult Holocaust novel *The Book Thief* or the cultish paranoia of Mark Danielewski's intricately self-protective *House of Leaves*; this is one of the ways in which morality enters into even the most stringently formalist ways of reading, and I will return later to the complex antagonisms and interdependencies that unite reading for the sentence and reading for the heart.

2

Lord Leighton, Liberace and the Advantages of Bad Writing

Helen DeWitt, Harry Stephen Keeler,
Lionel Shriver, George Eliot

These pages treat the inner workings of sentences and paragraphs as they function in novels. To read for the sentence
risks becoming trivial or pedantic: what about character, plot,
imagery, the host of other pleasures prose fiction lavishes upon
its readers? But the shape of any given sentence—its arc, to
use the visual metaphor; its cadence, to rank ear before eye—
produces part of its meaning, sometimes the most important
part. The aspects of meaning contributed by word choice, by
diction, by syntax are sometimes neglected by people who
write about novels, and this book is designed partly to redress
that balance, offering a modest manifesto in aid of reading
for the sentence. Sentences can be verbal artifacts of untold
complexity, and I am especially interested in ones that are
hidden, like Edgar Allan Poe's purloined letter, in plain view:

in novels, which tend to be thought of as being made up of larger units (scenes, chapters, episodes) rather than as the accumulation of a number of sentences large enough that one would not want to have to count them by hand.

The term *style* derives from the Latin *stilus*, a pointed instrument for writing. *Style* conjures up the little black dress, a world of haute couture and Audrey Hepburn, but it also invokes William Strunk Jr. and E. B. White's *Elements of Style* and the grammatical prescriptions of the style sheet; though grammar may seem less glamorous than fashion, *glamour* is etymologically speaking a corruption of *grammar*, by way of a set of related terms (*gramarye*, *grimoire*) that refer to a body of occult knowledge. The *Oxford English Dictionary* suggests that *style* may refer to the manner in which something is written, including a writer's characteristic mode of expression, but a pattern of tension soon emerges from its series of definitions. Is style merely something superficial, referring to features "which belong to form and expression rather than to the substance of the thought or the matter expressed"? Or do we instead adopt the wisdom embodied in the old adage "The style is the man," which implies that every aspect of character is written into each sentence a person writes?

My own suspicions gibe better with the second notion. Style is not extraneous, style is everything; one need not be a pure Wildean aesthete to adhere to such a view. To some extent I believe this is true for all writing, not just for literary writing, and I would use the word *temperament* to sum up the complex set of intellectual, emotional, political and cultural traits that make up a given person's identity as it is expressed in words. Temperament can be discerned with extraordinary clarity and economy in certain sentences or paragraphs ("The theatre is a better school of moral sentiments than churches"), and a reader's selection of which bits of a writer's work to foreground itself serves as one way of presenting an argument about that writer's deep nature. It has always seemed to me (but then I have the soul of a copy editor) that the sentence is the key to the heart: that sentences embody ethos in a way that renders deeply ingrained habits of thought visible to the naked eye. As a corollary, a particular passage's fissures and self-contradictions, its peculiar force or suppleness or stringency, may become the most interesting and revealing object of literary scrutiny, with style both subjecting itself to and facilitating acts of judgment. This way of reading may equally provide traction on the prose of writers such as Thomas Hobbes and Edward Gibbon and Ralph Waldo Emerson, but my self-imposed mandate here involves a more specific question about writing: what can be learned by attending closely to the sentences of some of the great imaginative fictions of the last couple hundred years?

This is a formalist project in the sense that I will focus very persistently on linguistic details, but I've already started to make the case for the ethical freight of formalism and its reading practices. There seems to me little point in considering style apart from morality, and Helen DeWitt's novel *The Last Samurai* offers an exceptionally clear and appealing version of the argument that style may itself serve as a kind of morality. The novel's two narrators are Sibylla Newman and her son Ludo, a child of prodigious intelligence and learning who is desperately eager for Sibylla to reveal the identity of his father, a well-known writer who impregnated Sibylla during a one-night stand that came about chiefly as a consequence of her being too polite to tell him what she really thought of his prose style. The pseudonym Sibylla gives to the writer in question is Liberace:

> Liberace the musician had a terrible facility and a terrible sincerity; what he played he played with feeling, whether it was Roll Out the Barrel or I'll Be Seeing You, and in sad pieces a tear would well up over the

mascara and drop to the silver diamanté of a velvet coat while the rings on his hands flashed up and down the keyboard, and in a thousand mirrors he would see the tear, the mascara, the rings, he would see himself seeing the mascara, the rings, the tear. All this could be found too in Liberace (the writer): the slick, buttery arpeggios, the self-regarding virtuosity as the clever ring-laden hands sparkled over the keys, the professional sincerity which found expressiveness for the cynical & the sentimental, for the pornographic, even for alienation & affectlessness.[1]

"He liked I expect the idea of effortless excellence, & being unable to combine the two had settled for the one he could be sure of," Sibylla concludes, aphoristically (Oscar Wilde is one of the talismans with which she wards off an existential despair). At Liberace's flat, she is horrified to note the presence of "a brand new book by Lord Leighton":

By Lord Leighton, of course, I don't mean the Hellenising late-Victorian painter of A Syracusan Bride Leading Wild Beasts in Procession and Greek Girls Playing at Ball, but the painterly American writer who is the spiritual heir of that artist. Lord Leighton (the painter) specialised in scenes of antiquity in which marvellous perplexities of drapery roamed the canvas, tarrying only in their travels to protect the modesty of a recruit from the Tyrone Power school of acting. His fault was not a lack of skill: it is the faultlessness of his skill which makes the paintings embarrassing to watch, so bare do they strip the mind of their creator. Only the pen of Lord Leighton the writer could do justice to the brush of Lord Leighton the painter, for just so did Lord Leighton (the writer) bring the most agitated emotions to an airless to a hushed to an unhurried while each word took on because there was all the time in the world for each word to take on the bloom which only a great Master can give to a word using his time to allow all unseemly energy to become aware of its nakedness and snatch gratefully at the fig leaf provided until all passion in the airlessness in the hush in the absence of hurry sank decently down in the slow death of motion to perpetual stasis: a character could not look, or step, or speak, without a gorgeous train of sentences swathing his poor stupid thoughts and unfolding in beautiful languor on the still and breathless air. (70–71)

Sibylla's war on cliché and bad writing is the crusade of a person who believes that human ethical life depends on the clear and effective practice of rational thought, including clarity of language (it is related to the argument Orwell made in "Politics and the English Language," but with a less political and more aesthetic and intellectual slant). Those gorgeous trains of sentences aren't just in bad taste, they're an offense against humanity, and style here is seen to be the repository of character, something we have an obligation to judge: to judge, and to cry out against when we find it wanting.

This version of the argument about style rests, really, on sensibility, a word I like because of the way it opens up more to ethos than style does while retaining the sense of what's at stake being a matter more of texture or tact or feel than first and foremost of ideas or arguments. The novelist Lydia Millet has made what seems to me a related argument, only this is the "hard" version, which goes further in terms of mandating an ethics of fictional subject matter as well as style. Millet took issue, in a piece published in the *Globe and Mail* in 2006, not so much with Alice Munro's canonization as "the Grande Dame of Canadian realism" as with the consequences of that canonization (in the *New Yorker*, Jonathan Franzen had recently called her "the best living writer in North America").[2] Her objection rested on the extent to which Munro's prose, so skillful and precise, makes "insistent choice of the purely personal, the proximate world of the self and its near relations," with the individual and his or her relationships with friends and family at the heart of this world's "cosmology" and even Munro's depiction of the land she knows so well serving as "a setting primarily for a specific subset of us, for the foibles and discoveries and preoccupations of the social self." The shortcoming of "the broader, dominant literary culture of realistic and personal fictions," Millet goes on to say, in which Munro leads and others follow, is that almost everything else "drops away entirely in favour of a massive foreground of people with problems":

> These problems are rarely starvation or war; they tend to be adultery or career disappointment, say, which leaves us with a literary culture whose preoccupation is not meaning or beauty, not right or wrong, not our philosophies or propensity for atrocities or corrupt churches and governments, but rather our sex lives, our social mistakes, our neighbourhood failures and sibling rivalries. Enlightenment humanism finds a kind of perfect expression here: If our deliberations about our personal lives, consisting of a near-infinite scrutiny of the tiny passages through which we move in relation to friends and lovers, constitutes the best calling of art, must such self-scrutiny not also be our own highest calling and rightful task?

I was caught up short when I first read this precisely because of how vividly and clearly it seemed to articulate something that has been on my mind as long as I have been reading short stories. The literary short story, in North America, suffers especially pervasively from the sort of self-absorption (to use the term literally rather than pejoratively, describing simply an involvement with individual self) that Millet discerns and deplores. I have always liked Muriel Spark especially because of how she bucks the trend of novelists being interested primarily in individuals in couples, traditional families, parents and children. Spark's novels tend to be set in schools and boardinghouses and convents—in short, in places where the fundamental unit is not the couple or the nuclear or extended family but rather the small- to medium-sized group: Spark is the great novelist of small groups! In contrast, the tradition of John Updike and John Cheever and Alice Munro seems to me excessively centered on an aspect of life that would seem to be woefully narrow, at least in the greater context of political struggle and institutional service and global migration and passionate religious belief or intellectual commitment, to name just a few of the things that make lives interesting.

This is a digression, but it happened that in the same month that Millet weighed in on the problem of tiny passages, Joan Acocella published an encomium in the *New Yorker* on Alice McDermott's latest novel. I must confess that I have never read a word of McDermott's fiction beyond the bits Acocella quoted in this piece, but those passages, eminently skillful and quoted lovingly by Acocella, aroused my deepest suspicion and dislike.[3] Here the protagonist is coming out of lunchtime Mass in New York just after World War II:

> Leaving the church, she felt the wind rise, felt the pinprick of pebble and grit against her stockings and her cheeks. . . . And all before her, the lunch-hour crowd bent under the April sun and into the bitter April wind, jackets flapping and eyes squinting, or else skirts pressed to the backs of legs and jacket hems pressed to bottoms. And trailing them, outrunning them, skittering along the

gutter and the sidewalk and the low gray steps of the church, banging into ankles and knees and one another, scraps of paper, newspapers, candy wrappers, what else?—office memos? shopping lists? The paper detritus that she had somewhere read, or had heard it said, trails armies, or was it (she had seen a photograph) the scraps of letters and wrappers and snapshots that blow across battlefields after all but the dead had fled?[4]

I'm not crazy about the rather grandiose rhetorical gesture in the last part of the passage, but that's neither here nor there. What struck me was that this is a kind of language I strongly associate with the literary short story (though obviously novels are written in this mode as well, and this is a novel rather than a story); the problem I have with it—the thing that makes it leave me cold—is that it is so much concerned with sensation at the expense of thought or even emotion. I'm not enthusiastic about that aspect of Woolf's writing either— it seems to me that the challenge the modernists imposed on themselves, of radically extending what sentences could do vis-à-vis the physiological moment-to-moment intensity of lived experience, was not in the end a really fruitful one. I find myself not very interested even in my *own* sensations, and not at all interested in sensations and physical observations sup- posedly filtered through the consciousness of this character of McDermott's. I would rather know what the character *thinks*, thinks about something interesting or funny or important or irrelevant. The abstract quality of this perceptiveness about scraps of paper and skirts pressed to the backs of legs (the word "skittering" strikes me in this context as excessively and self-consciously literary) isn't *sensible*; it's not funny, either, and I expect it's really the sensation-freighted-with-significance thing that alienates me rather than the focus on sensation in itself. This is always the problem I have reading Alice Munro or William Trevor. Both are wonderfully good writers, and if I am going to read that kind of thing, I would take Munro or Trevor over almost anyone else I can think of, and yet I find myself as a reader having really no *need* for that kind of thing.

What am I proposing as a model instead, or rather what sort of fiction attracts me as strongly as this repels me, in the cool core sense of pushing me away? I would offer two different answers, the first slightly perverse and the second more in earnest. My perverse counterexample to the McDermott-Munro-Trevor school of fiction-writing, a writer as profoundly antithetical to that mode as anything one can imagine, is the cult favorite Harry Stephen Keeler. Keeler has some passionate detractors. Crime fiction publisher and provocateur Otto Penzler, writing for the *New York Sun*, called Keeler "the worst writer in the world": "Keeler is to good literature as rectal cancer is to good health. He makes the J. D. Robb novels seem as if they were written by Shakespeare. Given the choice of reading three Keeler novels back to back or being imprisoned in an Iranian jail, you'd need to think about it."[5] Penzler's hyperbole is counterbalanced by the equally hyperbolic advocacy of a coterie of prominent Keelerites. Paul Collins edited *The Riddle of the Traveling Skull* (1934) for a McSweeney's reissue in 2005, and the novelist and critic Ed Park is another influential supporter (his younger son is named Keeler!). While I would not call myself a full-blown Keelerite, I am undoubtedly taken with Keeler's prose style. Certain novels are famous for having invented their own idioms: *1984*, *A Clockwork Orange*, *The Catcher in the Rye*. Ernest Hemingway and Raymond Chandler both developed highly recognizable idioms, and so did Dickens; it would be a mistake to think of this as a twentieth-century phenomenon, as on some level any really good novel does this, so that it is only the case that some examples are more exaggerated or obviously remarkable than others.

Keeler's idiom is so strange as almost to amount to a new dialect of English. *The Riddle of the Traveling Skull* is dense with vivid but peculiar colloquialisms ("two shakes of a lamb-let's tail," "24-carat thoroughbred"), and Keeler makes very odd use of the dash to signal thinking. Here are a few sentences that give the feel of his prose:

Canada is as much of a refuge for you as—as a Wisconsin lumber camp is for a lost virgin.

My forehead was so corrugated, as I could sense by feeling alone, that an Eskimo's fur coat, sprinkled with nothing but Lux, could have been washed on it.

Either as a detective I was a good sofa-pillow crocheter, or else I was playing in the identical luck of the piccolo player when the eccentric millionaire filled up the instruments of each member of the German band with $5 gold pieces.

I held up that costermonger dummy significantly.[6]

It would not be a good thing if everybody wrote like Keeler. But his use of simile and comparison is strikingly imaginative, almost grotesquely so. His inset references are strange for reasons at once verbal and substantive, conspiring to elicit an unusually strongly cognitive readerly response. The stuttered "as" in that first sentence makes a comparison that complicates rather than clarifying, as similes are generally supposed to do; the "corrugated" forehead of the second example literalizes the conventional synecdoche in which a furrowed brow is supposed to represent thinking, grounding the image by way of a bizarre far-flung allusion to the now-outdated technology of the washboard. The third example does something similar to the first, insofar as what are grammatically represented as alternatives actually offer the same thing twice rather than proposing two possibilities differing in their fundamentals; the image of the German band, the piccolo and so forth has something of the same particularizing strangeness as the Lux-sprinkled fur coat of the preceding example. Of the final example, I will only say that I am very certain this particular sequence of seven words has never appeared in any other literary work: the noun *costermonger dummy* shares that strangeness so characteristically at once verbal and physical, with the odd placement of the adverb at the end of the sentence compounding the effect. This is style for its own sake, a demented high-energy arabesque not really directed toward anything other than the performance of a sensibility. Many readers will prefer McDermott to Keeler. But what this style has going for it that McDermott's sort of prose doesn't is a sheer verbal inventiveness and originality that delights me far more than the tastefully modulated sentences of a Munro or a Trevor.

My second example lacks the lightness of touch, the wayward strangeness of the Keeler passages. It is drawn from Lionel Shriver's novel *The Post-Birthday World*, which takes a set of characters and recounts two divergent stories for them, fates and futures that split off depending on a choice made by the protagonist, Irina, on her birthday. I have already suggested, by way of those quotations from *The Last Samurai*, that it is worth asking what it means to talk about style as something moralized. Beyond the linguistic or strictly literary aspects of a novel's style, is it just a fallacy to think that styles encapsulate moral orientations toward characters, or is it fair to think of diction itself as intrinsically wrapped up with acts of moral judgment? The reason *The Post-Birthday World* so clearly illuminates this question arises from Shriver's decision to tell two stories that run on parallel tracks. Consider these two passages, the first from the post-birthday world in which Irina has kissed another man (her live-in boyfriend,

Lawrence, has just arrived home the next evening, and Irina's in the kitchen cutting him a piece of the pie she baked the day before for his homecoming—the pie originates in the "single" world before Irina's life story split into alternate strands), the second from the world in which she refrained from doing so:

Leadenly, Irina removed the pie from the fridge. Chilling for under two hours, it wasn't completely set. With any luck the egg in the filling had cooked thoroughly enough that the pie's having been left out on the counter for a full day wasn't deadly. Well, she herself wouldn't manage more than a bite. (She'd not been able to eat a thing since that last spoonful of green-tea ice cream. Though there had been another cognac around noon . . .) The slice she cut for herself was so slight that it fell over. For Lawrence, she hacked off a far larger piece—Lawrence was always watching his weight—than she knew he wanted. The wedge sat fat and stupid on the plate; the filling drooled. Ramsey didn't need admiration of his snooker game, and Lawrence didn't need pie.[7]

And here's the post-birthday world in which Irina has virtuously suppressed her sexual attraction to Ramsey (Lawrence has just criticized her for having had a drink before he got home):

Scrutinized for signs of inebriation and disgusted with herself for having overimbibed the night before, in the kitchen Irina poured herself an abstemious half-glass of white wine. She pulled out the pie, which after chilling for a full day was nice and firm, and made picture-perfect slices that might have joined the duplicitous array of photographs over a Woolworth's lunch counter. She shouldn't have any herself; oddly, she'd snacked all afternoon. But countless chunks of cheddar had failed to quell a ravenous appetite, so tonight she cut herself a wide wedge, whose filling blushed a fleshy, labial pink. This she crowned with a scoop of vanilla. Lawrence's slice she carefully made more modest, with only a dollop of ice cream. No gesture was truly generous that made him feel fat. (69)

Shriver's sentences very effectively express two different mindsets or orientations on Irina's part: in the first pair of paragraphs, there is a satirical self-loathing energy that anticipates a set of unexpected but liberating choices that "this" Irina will go on to make, while the second example shows Irina dutifully submitting the force of her own personality to the shape of sentences that are as steady, sedate and self-concluding as the other sentences are oblique or destabilizing. Neither passage depicts a moment of significance or even centrally of self-reflection, but the moral implications of Irina's choice are written into every turn of phrase; Shriver wants to show us two strikingly different orientations toward a character's state of being, though the schematic nature of the opposition risks rendering both modes parodic or reductive. It is impossible to tell whether that second passage is inadvertently clumsy or deliberately satirical, and it can be said that in certain respects Lionel Shriver is a bad writer—but a bad writer in the sense that George Eliot, too, is a bad writer. *Middlemarch* is both unparalleled in its greatness and full of sentences that make me cringe, not because of the insights they express but because of the words in which those thoughts are couched. At such times, Eliot's style has about it something graceless or embarrassing:

The excessive feeling manifested would alone have been highly disturbing to Mr Casaubon, but there were other reasons why Dorothea's words were among the most cutting and irritating to him that she could have been impelled to use. She was as blind to his inward troubles as he to hers; she had not yet learned those hidden conflicts in her husband which claim our pity. She had not yet listened patiently to his heart-beats, but only felt that her own was beating violently. In Mr Casaubon's ear, Dorothea's voice gave loud emphatic iteration to those muffled suggestions of consciousness which it was possible to explain as mere fancy, the illusion of exaggerated sensitiveness: always when such suggestions are unmistakably repeated from without, they are resisted as cruel and unjust. We are angered even by the full acceptance of our humiliating confessions—how much more by hearing in hard distinct syllables from the lips of a near observer, those confused murmurs which we try to call morbid, and strive against as if they were the oncoming of numbness![8]

"Those hidden conflicts . . . which claim our pity": ugh! That "our" is intolerably smug; it is either presumptuous ("you the reader and I the narrator know that which Dorothea does not") or sanctimonious (the "we" of philanthropy and charitable condescension). I don't like the word "iteration" here—it seems pretentious or overly technical—and I dislike even more the move after the colon to aphoristic generalization: it may be true, but there's something coy or even annoying about the smug diction of the pronouncement. It can be said throughout, though, that intellectual muscle and a sort of temperamental obtrusiveness do the work for Eliot that a perfectly impeccable style might do for another novelist (an Austen or a Flaubert). Many of the turns of phrase the narrator offers have something arch or self-satisfied about them—I have singled out some of the ones I especially hate—and yet the force of the insights is unparalleled, so that the blocky embarrassments of the language perfectly set off the intelligence of the psychological commentary. It could not be a better passage if it were more tastefully inoffensive; it is perfect exactly as it is. This passage sums up for me the strange allure of *Middlemarch*, a book that would not be nearly so brilliant if it were not so frequently and grotesquely ponderous in its locutions, and it is a strength rather than a weakness that Shriver can be said to share something of Eliot's badness.

3

Mouthy Pleasures and the Problem of Momentum

Gary Lutz, *Lolita*, Lydia Davis, Jonathan Lethem

In an essay called "The Sentence Is a Lonely Place," Gary Lutz tells the story of his discovery of a group of books "in which virtually every sentence had the force and feel of a climax, in which almost every sentence was a vivid extremity of language, an abruption, a definitive inquietude," books (most or all of them edited by Gordon Lish) whose writers "recognized the sentence as the one true theater of endeavor, as the place where writing comes to a point and attains its ultimacy."[1] These books reveal to Lutz that he himself wants to produce "narratives of steep verbal topography, narratives in which the sentence is a complete, portable solitude, a minute immediacy of consummated language—the sort of sentence that, even when liberated from its receiving context, impresses itself upon the eye and the ear as a totality, an omnitude, unto itself." He calls this kind of sentence "an outcry combining the acoustical elegance of the aphorism with the force and utility of the load-bearing, tractional sentence of more or less conventional narrative," a description that pairs these two aspects of the ideal sentence in a way that emphasizes the tension between self-contained aphoristic stasis on the one hand and the going-somewhere aspect of fiction on the other. A tractor, though we tend to think of it mostly as an agricultural vehicle, can actually be anything that draws or pulls something else (the "tractor beam" of *Star Trek*). Thus "load-bearing, tractional" are basically synonymous, the pair of terms offered partly for emphasis but also to give Lutz's own substantive and load-bearing sentence an allegiance it can wear on its sleeve: the gratuitous pairing, with that obtrusive comma, tips the sentence toward the stylized, the nonfunctional.

Sentences of the sort that Lutz praises are experienced through the mouth as well as the ear and the eye. Lutz's own fiction has a *chewy* quality, his diction strangely combining a feeling of the inevitable with near-extraplanetary strangeness. Here are three paragraphs from "Waking Hours," from the collection *Stories in the Worst Way:*

> I was in receipt of the mothered-down version of the kid every other Saturday. The bus would make an unscheduled stop in front of the building where I lived, and then out he would come, morseled in an oversized down jacket, all candy-breathed from the ride. I would drive us to a family restaurant where we would slot into seats opposite each other and he would ask me the questions his mother had asked him to ask. I had a quick-acting, pesticidal answer for every one.
>
> When the food arrived—kiddie-menu concentrates for him, an overproportioned hamburger for me—I would tilt the conversation toward him, maybe a little

too steeply. I would want to poach on the life inside him, whatever it was. He would splay his hands on the table-top, arms slat-straight, crutching himself up.

After lunch, in the undemanding dark of a movie the-ater where he goggled at some stabby, Roman-numeraled sequel, I would plug my ears and loot my own heart.[2]

Lutz has an unusual sense of adjective and verb. "Mothered-down," "morseled"—these words don't exactly make for tongue-twisters, but they linger in the mouth nonetheless, just as juxtapositions like "candy-breathed" (a tricky coinage that visually invites misreading via the more familiar past-tense "breathed," with its voiced *th*) or "quick-acting, pesticidal" insist on a rhythm that disrupts the reader's own likely sense of the natural motion of sentences. ("Quick-acting, pesti-cidal" echoes the rhythms of "load-bearing, tractional," a verbal pattern for which Lutz shows a strong preference.) The "tilt" of the conversation is rendered almost more literal than figurative by the further application of the adverb "steeply," and the passage is full of verbs not unusual in themselves but distinctly odd in their application here: "slot," "poach," "crutching," "goggled" (the middle two of these four also come with unusual prepositions: "poach on," "crutching him-self up"). These words call attention to themselves by their sound (in particular by their combinations of consonants) as well as their meaning. So does the clever and slightly painful formulation "some stabby, Roman-numeraled sequel": almost too smart for its own good, the expression allows for a small eruption of pain or pathos through the irony. This sort of movie is "stabby" not just because people get stabbed in hor-ror movies (and the perpendicular lines of the Roman numer-als here come to seem almost weapons themselves, knives or javelins) but because it is the sort of movie fathers sundered from their sons inflict upon themselves; the "s" of "stabby" and the liquid "-aled" of "numeraled" get neatly wrapped up together in the final word "sequel."

Lutz takes an unusually extreme position, of course, on the merits of the tractional versus the topographic. In an interview, Lutz once said, in response to a question from Daniel Long about whether syntax was really sufficient unto itself or whether his notions of story and character might perhaps be beneficially expanded,

> I just do what my nervous system wants done or allows me to do. It is not in my nature to care about plots. I do not see storylines in life. Life hits me by the instant. My writing is a record of one instant after another, with causality mostly drained away. I am trying to describe how life and the world look and feel to me. The world has already been plentifully described otherwise. I have nothing to add to those descriptions and see no reason to try. Characterization is no concern of mine, either. The last thing I want to do is to bring somebody new into words. I practice birth control of a typographical kind.[3]

Language need not be emphasized so much at the expense of the traditional pleasures of story, even given a commitment to acoustical elegance. The famous opening of one of the twentieth century's best-loved novels offers a near-perfect invitation to perform this sort of reading on the tongue. Here are the first three paragraphs of Vladimir Nabokov's *Lolita*:

> Lolita, light of my life, fire of my loins. My sin, my soul. Lo-lee-ta: the tip of the tongue taking a trip of three steps down the palate to tap, at three, on the teeth. Lo. Lee. Ta.

> She was Lo, plain Lo, in the morning, standing four
> feet ten in one sock. She was Lola in slacks. She was
> Dolly at school. She was Dolores on the dotted line. But
> in my arms she was always Lolita.
>
> Did she have a precursor? She did, indeed she did.
> In point of fact, there might have been no Lolita at all
> had I not loved, one summer, a certain initial girl-child.
> In a princedom by the sea. Oh when? About as many
> years before Lolita was born as my age was that sum-
> mer. You can always count on a murderer for a fancy
> prose style.[4]

The relationship between sound and sense interests narrator
Humbert Humbert, and the obtrusive presence of his own
tongue on the page prompts uncomfortable mimicry in the
reader's mouth.

It is not only elaborate or fancy sentences that call for this
sort of reading through the mouth. Nabokov and Lutz are
similar in their preference for using words almost as neolo-
gisms, attending to their literal meanings and origins and then
wrenching them sideways, like the knight's move in chess, to
create unexpected and often disorienting new sense. But very
plain sentences can also be "chewy." Here is Lydia Davis's
short story "Boring Friends," in its entirety (it is from the collection *Samuel Johnson Is Indignant*):

> We know only four boring people. The rest of our
> friends we find very interesting. However, most of the
> friends we find interesting find us boring: the most
> interesting find us the most boring. The few who are
> somewhere in the middle, with whom there is recipro-
> cal interest, we distrust: at any moment, we feel, they
> may become too interesting for us, or we too interesting
> for them.[5]

Davis has taken concision as a storytelling practice perhaps as far as it can go without becoming mere gimmick (I am thinking of the fashion for the six-word life story, licensed on the Internet by an example that is attributed to Hemingway, though I doubt it originated with him: "For sale: baby shoes, never worn"). The title story of that collection of Davis's, for instance, reads in its entirety as follows, with the colon marking the break between title and story, "Samuel Johnson Is Indignant: that Scotland has so few trees."[6] Davis's sentences are as "mouthy" as Lutz's, in a different way, but I do not know that the effect could be enjoyably extended (the counter-example of *Lolita*'s opening notwithstanding) over a fiction made up of tens of thousands of words; at any rate, a novel is likely to display more varied diction than either Lutz's or Davis's much more compressed stories.

I can think of a few recent novels that offer "mouthy" pleasures—the almost physical sense, in the reader's body, of each word and sentence being formed for one's sensory delectation—without compromising the traditional narrative pleasures of long-form fiction. James Lasdun and A. L. Kennedy, for instance, both seem to me to work equally effectively in the short story and the novel formats. But my best example of a contemporary long novel that offers not just the deep plea-sures I associate with nineteenth-century realist fiction (*David Copperfield, Middlemarch*) but also the "mouthy" pleasures of a Davis or a Lutz is Jonathan Lethem's *The Fortress of Solitude*. I find the narrative consistently and mesmerizingly perfect in its diction, immensely satisfying in the exact place-ment of the words even as the sentences are also effectively tractional, load-bearing:

> Mingus fished in his lining for his El Marko, a Magic Marker consisting of a puglike glass bottle stoppered with a fat wick of felt. Purple ink sloshed inside the

tiny screw-top bottle, staining the glass in curtains of color. Mingus drew out a safety pin and stuck the felt in a dozen places, *pinning it out* he called it, until the ink bled so freely it stained the light skin at his palm, then the green cuff of his oversize jacket. Dylan felt a quiver of the pleasure he associated with his father's tiny brushes, with Spirograph cogs and skully caps.[7]

A hyperawareness of language runs throughout this paragraph, which follows the protagonist Dylan's consciousness very closely: it is Dylan who is struck by the vivid phrase *pinning it out*, Dylan who notices and marks to himself in language these physical objects with their striking double existence in language and in the world itself. One of the things I like most in this novel is its portrait of Dylan's awful friend Arthur Lomb, his ally in an as-yet-ungentrified 1970s Brooklyn where two white boys painfully stand out. Arthur Lomb's speech is transcribed in all of its cartoonishness:

Only thing that matters is the test for Stuyvesant. Just math and science. Flunk English, who gives? The whole report card thing's a joke, always was. I haven't gone to gym class once. You know Jesus Maldonado? He said he'd break my arm like a Pixy Stix if he caught me alone in the locker room. Gym's suicide, frankly. I'm not stripping down to my underwear anywhere inside the four walls of this school, I'm just not. If I have to BM, I hold it until after school. (124)

Mel Brooks's funniest film is *The Producers*, then *Young Frankenstein* or *Blazing Saddles*. Terri Garr is hot. I feel sorry for any kid who hasn't seen *The Producers*. My dad took me to all the humor movies. The best Panther is probably *Return*. The best Woody is *Everything You Always Wanted to Know About Sex*. (126)

This sort of extended monologue, though, which allows the reader to locate Arthur Lomb (he is always called by his full name) on the taxonomic map of human personality and to judge him as harshly and precisely as he tabulates and judges cultural products, leads into an extraordinarily humane and perceptive reflection about Dylan's relationship to his impossible friend:

> Positioning, positioning, Arthur Lomb was forever positioning himself, making his views known, aligning on some index no one would ever consult. Here was Dylan's burden, his cross: the accumulated knowledge of Arthur Lomb's smug policies on every possible question. The cross was Dylan's to bear, he knew, because his own brain boiled with pedantry, with too-eager trivia ready to burst loose at any moment. So in enduring Arthur Lomb Dylan had been punished in advance for the possibility of being a bore.

The first sentence employs two triplets—the word "positioning" appears three times, but its third use also represents the first term in a second threesome ("positioning," "making," "aligning"). The sentence would feel quite different if Lethem had chosen to use a semicolon or colon after the phrase "positioning himself"; the comma is less judgmental in this case than either of those other punctuation marks. Each successive sentence unfolds with a similarly sharp sense of how the comma can be used to capture the texture of thought: "Dylan's burden, his cross"; "with pedantry, with too-eager trivia." Then, after three sentences in which phrases proliferate, comes a final sentence of straight summation, a sentence

33

that lacks any punctuation other than the period at its end and that can be thought of as existing in a relationship to the preceding block of text that would be marked, if it were all one long sentence, by a colon, the colon being the form of punctuation that most clearly puts one set of things in apposition to another. This invisible or notional colon offers a counterweight to the earlier colon and its despairing identification of "the accumulated knowledge of Arthur Lomb's smug policies" as Dylan's cross. The passage's effectiveness depends to a great extent on the shape and cadence of the sentences rather than on the incorporation of "mouthy" nouns; that affinity with the mouthy is more clearly on view in the previous passage I quoted, with words like "puglike," "wick" and "sloshed" and the evocative listing of colors and artist's tools. In short, Lethem is able to mobilize a wider range of effects than either Davis or Lutz, and *The Fortress of Solitude* maintains a storytelling momentum that invites the comparison to nineteenth-century realist fiction (Dickens, Honoré de Balzac); it is finally a limitation, I think, however much it attracts me, that Lutz and Davis appeal to the reader by way of the emotional privation conveyed in the bald sequence of words grounded in the mouth.

4

The Acoustical Elegance of Aphorism

Kafka, Fielding, Austen, Flaubert

It is possible that I have read *Pride and Prejudice* as many as fifty times. At eight or nine, I had a battered mass-market garage-sale paperback, its cover depicting a supercilious blonde bonneted Elizabeth Bennet looking slyly away from Mr. Darcy, their appearances puzzlingly at odds with the film stills included inside from the 1940 Hollywood adaptation with Greer Garson and Laurence Olivier. I was young enough not to understand the extent to which Austen wants us to notice Mr. Bennet's shortcomings as a father (the absurdity of Mary's aspirations to philosophy also mostly passed me by), but that didn't prevent the novel from becoming at once a love object and an object of obsessive scrutiny. It might be that I learned more about sentences and forms of narration from *Pride and Prejudice* than from any other source. I remember the excitement of teaching the novel, as a graduate student assistant, in a Penguin edition that gave me almost the illusion of reading the book for the first time. I have taught it seven or eight times since, and written about it at regular intervals, but each time I reread it, I notice at least one thing I have never seen before, a striking formulation or a curious juxtaposition or an unresolved ambiguity.

Austen's prose is remarkable in being at the same time supremely stylized, crafted, controlled and also exceptionally productive of identification and empathy; indeed, her novels produce an intensity of author-love (and sometimes author-hate) that makes them unusually difficult to teach, if the goal is to consider the workings of sentences and paragraphs, modes of narration and authorial voice. A novel such as *Emma*, though the precision and ingenuity of its language may periodically stop the reader short, invites reading by the scene or the chapter or the volume: reading in gulps. What happens when the kind of very close reading demanded by the prose of Lutz or Davis is leveled on sentences that are on the face of things far more evidently tractional and load-bearing than most of the ones I have looked at so far? "Emma Woodhouse, handsome, clever, and rich, with a comfortable home and happy disposition, seemed to unite some of the best blessings of existence; and had lived nearly twenty-one years in the world with very little to distress or vex her."[1]

Emma's opening sentence could almost be the beginning of a real-world fairy tale; perhaps only the verb "seemed" and the ostentatiously positive sequence of traits ("handsome, clever, and rich") hint that there will be some satirical or ironic undermining of the premise so straightforwardly asserted. (Austen famously promised in a letter, writing of this novel's title character, that she intended to create a heroine "whom no-one but myself will much like.") The narrative continues in this way:

She was the youngest of the two daughters of a most affectionate, indulgent father, and had, in consequence of her sister's marriage, been mistress of his house from a very early period. Her mother had died too long ago for her to have more than an indistinct remembrance of her caresses, and her place had been supplied by an excellent woman as governess, who had fallen little short of a mother in affection.

Sixteen years had Miss Taylor been in Mr. Woodhouse's family, less as a governess than a friend, very fond of both daughters, but particularly of Emma. Between *them* it was more the intimacy of sisters. Even before Miss Taylor had ceased to hold the nominal office of governess, the mildness of her temper had hardly allowed her to impose any restraint; and the shadow of authority being now long passed away, they had been living together as friend and friend very mutually attached, and Emma doing just what she liked; highly esteeming Miss Taylor's judgment, but directed chiefly by her own.

I'm interested here in the tension between the narrative sentences and the aphoristic ones—between sentences of acoustical elegance and ones that are primarily tractional and load-bearing, to use Lutz's terms. These paragraphs are primarily load-bearing, filling in background and contextualizing the character with a sketch of her family history; the diction is precise without being explicitly satirical, although it verges here and there on irony, particularly in the last line of the penultimate paragraph. Austen offers a sharp judgmental summing-up in the phrase "Emma doing just what she liked," then unpacks Emma's choices into an opposition that is structurally reminiscent of satire, if not actually satirical, delineating a dynamic tension between Emma's "highly esteeming" the governess's judgment while being "directed chiefly by her own."

It is the next paragraph, though, whose rhythms and structure will become markedly aphoristic: "The real evils indeed of Emma's situation were the power of having rather too much her own way, and a disposition to think a little too well of herself; these were the disadvantages which threatened alloy to her many enjoyments. The danger, however, was at present so unperceived, that they did not by any means rank as misfortunes with her."

The broad summing-up in the first sentence is not a satirical judgment as such, though the lurking irony is heightened by the precise and unusual word choice "threatened alloy" (the precision itself, not just the slightly surprising use of "alloy" as an abstract noun rather than as the more familiar verb, signals that something is happening beyond what's said). The final sentence, though, undoubtedly has the ring of satire. It's not a symmetrically balanced sentence in the classic manner of the eighteenth-century British couplet ("Good nature and good sense must ever join; / To err is human, to forgive, divine")—it ends with a preposition-plus-pronoun pair ("with her") that unseats the whole thing. The word "however" sets this sentence on the other end of a see-saw from the one that precedes it, and its shorter length does not preclude its having an equivalent or greater amount of pull than the one it follows. The notion that Emma's disadvantages "did not by any means rank as misfortunes with her" *at present* sets up the likelihood of a future in which this state of affairs will be inverted, a future made possible in the sentence precisely by the narrator's shift into an aphoristic mode.

What exactly do I mean when I say *aphorism*? One way of defining the term is to give a few of the "maxims," though the terms *maxim* and *aphorism* are not always interchangeable, of the seventeenth-century French writer François de La

Rochefoucauld. La Rochefoucauld's formulations are sharp, cynical, abbreviated, with a satirical dynamism that springs from the unexpected and often highly ingenious coupling of terms: "Hypocrisy is the tribute which vice pays to virtue." Here is Jonathan Swift's translation of another of La Rochefoucault's maxims: "In the Adversity of our best Friends, we find something that doth not displease us."[2] The rubric of aphorism covers a whole family of associated forms, all relatively brief and gnomic, from the self-explanatory folk proverb ("Haste makes waste"; "A rolling stone gathers no moss") to William Blake's troubling and enigmatic proverbs in *The Marriage of Heaven and Hell* ("Drive your cart and your plow over the bones of the dead"; "The cistern contains: the fountain overflows") or to Franz Kafka's lovely and elusive Zürau aphorisms. La Rochefoucauld may provide the template for the aphorism—sharp, cynical, interested in human nature—but my favorite aphorisms of Kafka's serve less as sharp assertions about human nature and the human world than as self-contained elliptical parables, their feel not satirical so much as mythic:

> Leopards break into the temple and drink all the sacrificial vessels dry; it keeps happening; in the end, it can be calculated in advance and is incorporated into the ritual

> The animal twists the whip out of its master's grip and whips itself to become its own master—not knowing that this is only a fantasy, produced by a new knot in the master's whiplash.

> The crows like to insist a single crow is enough to destroy heaven. This is incontestably true, but it says nothing about heaven, because heaven is just another way of saying: the impossibility of crows.[3]

Strikingly, although things happen here (parables often have a narrative component), these small chunks of prose are not chronologically structured stories—the tense is that of a habitual or ongoing present, lending a timeless quality (legendary rather than historical in its associations) to the worlds they create.

The *Oxford English Dictionary* defines an aphorism, in the first place, as a definition or concise statement of a scientific principle, and by extension as "any principle or precept expressed in few words; a short pithy sentence containing a truth of general import; a maxim." The maxim or aphorism is a self-contained form (Kafka's short parables are not set into longer narratives; they stand on their own), but an aphoristic sentence can also punctuate or give piquancy to a longer paragraph of prose. Henry Fielding relies extensively on this technique. When Squire Allworthy decides to take in the illegitimate foundling Tom Jones and raise him as his own child, his sister, Mrs. Bridget, orders a suitable nursery to be set up, something she cannot do without complaining that "for her part, she could not help thinking it was an encouragement to vice; but that she knew too much of the obstinacy of mankind to oppose any of their ridiculous humours" (alluding to the supposed obstinacy of her brother, Allworthy, perhaps the sweetest-tempered character in the book):

With Reflections of this Nature she usually, as has been hinted, accompanied every Act of Compliance with her Brother's Inclinations; and surely nothing could more contribute to heighten the Merit of this Compliance, than a declaration that she knew, at the same Time, the Folly and Unreasonableness of those Inclinations to which she submitted. Tacit Obedience implies no Force upon the Will, and, consequently, may be easily, and without any Pains, preserved; but when a Wife, a Child, a Relation, or a Friend, performs what we desire, with Grumbling and Reluctance, with Expressions of Dislike and Dissatisfaction, the manifest Difficulty which they undergo, must greatly enhance the Obligation.

As this is one of those deep Observations which very few Readers can be supposed capable of making themselves, I have thought proper to lend them my Assistance; but this is a Favour rarely to be expected in the Course of my Work. Indeed, I shall seldom or never so indulge him, unless in such Instances as this, where nothing but the Inspiration with which we Writers are gifted, can possibly enable any one to make the Discovery.[4]

Mrs. Bridget's own original pronouncement—the words that prompt this authorial digression—is not allowed the dignity of aphorism. She utters a stream of commonplaces, and by giving them in the third person, the narrator minimizes the chance of Mrs. Bridget's formulations posing any threat to the authority of his own aphoristic style. The commentary of the subsequent paragraph begins with an observation that leads into a declaration about human nature that will be unfolded and elaborated in the succeeding sentence. This is classic irony, in the sense that the words work to establish a meaning opposite to what's said: rather than heightening the merit of compliance, such grumbling would more properly detract from it. Not content to leave the point at this, the narrator regroups and reformulates the argument in less sharply ironic and more broadly comical terms: Fielding uses repetition and listing ("a Wife, A Child, a Relation, or a Friend," "with Grumbling and Reluctance, with Expressions of Dislike and Dissatisfaction") to ramp up the joke, lest the reader be in any danger of missing the absurdity of the conclusion.

The subsequent paragraph represents an even more grandiose detour on the narrator's part, and the authorial persona here in many respects has less in common with the usual sort of first-person narrator than with the wide-ranging summing-up voice of third-person omniscient narration. The narrator doesn't mean it ironically when he says that few readers can be supposed capable of making this observation themselves—he's more delusional than that, and the observation not so "deep" as he supposes, with irony emerging from Fielding's orientation toward the narrator rather than from the narrator's toward the reader. His boast of "Inspiration" and his assertion of brotherhood in a group designated as "we Writers" harks back to the voice of the projector/hack writer who narrates Swift's brilliant and disorienting prose satire *A Tale of a Tub*. The legacy of the generation of writers that included Swift and Pope would remain very strong not just for Fielding but for Austen as well, though her novels were not written until the early years of the nineteenth century, roughly a hundred years after the beginning of Britain's Augustan age: Augustan because of the ways (in literature and politics) it reminded participants and onlookers of the Rome of Horace and Juvenal under the rule of Augustus. Britain's own period of empire, prosperity and power was deemed a second Augustan age not least because of the fact that satire had come to be considered the dominant— perhaps even the most prestigious—literary mode. The great writers of this period learned from La Rochefoucauld and other seventeenth-century French writers (Nicolas Boileau in particular) their mastery over irony, antithesis and the pointed form of the rhymed couplet. Satire ceased to be the dominant literary mode as the century progressed, but the sounds and rhythms of satire continued to inflect all sorts of prose as well as poetry. Even the social thought of Enlightenment giants like David Hume and Adam Smith can be seen as having a fundamentally ironic or paradoxical cast of thought, at the level of the sentence as well as of the broader arguments: Bernard Mandeville's notorious satire *The Fable of the Bees*, whose subtitle was *Private Vices, Publick Benefits*, was loathed by Adam Smith, but Mandeville's basic insight about how the vice of luxury at the individual level contributes to prosperity at the national level motivates some of Smith's own economic thought as well.

Irony, as in the passage from *Tom Jones*, may start out symmetrical or balanced but is appealingly prone to destabilizing swerves, away from the merely scathing observation or the devastating summing-up toward compassion or delusion or any one of a number of different affects. Consider these sentences from Samuel Johnson's *Life of Pope* (though it is biography, not satire, it is a biography of one of England's great satirical writers, and Johnson brings to bear on Alexander Pope's story a set of tools that include irony, paradox and aphorism):

> He tried all styles, and many subjects. He wrote a comedy, a tragedy, an epick poem, with panegyricks on all the princes of Europe; and, as he confesses, *thought himself the greatest genius that ever was.* Self-confidence is the first requisite to great undertakings; he, indeed, who forms his opinion of himself in solitude, without knowing the powers of other men, is very liable to errour; but it was the felicity of Pope to rate himself at his real value.[5]

Johnson dislikes aspects of Pope's personality but is scrupulously fair about his poetry, here and elsewhere in the *Life of Pope*; quoting Pope's own mocking-but-still-self-aggrandizing youthful self-assessment, Johnson is moved to offer a generalization ("Self-confidence is the first requisite to great undertakings"), then a blow (ironic in its diction but still devastating in its judgment) at those who rate themselves too high, before reining in the verbal aggression and retracting some (not all) of the implied criticism of the poet's character. The lightly ironized diction (the Latinate "felicity," for instance) has no specific target but contributes to give the reader a sense of the relative detachment of Johnson's critical judgment, so that the irony can be considered as being only partly at Pope's expense.

The opening line of D. A. Miller's essay "No One Is Alone," in the book called *Jane Austen, or The Secret of Style*, offers a singular provocation: "Of that godlike authority which we think of as the default mode of narration in the traditional novel," Miller writes, "Jane Austen may well be the *only* English example."[6] The narrators of Henry Fielding and William Thackeray and George Eliot, he asserts, are all associated with human characters, each of whom has at least implicitly a sex and a social position in which the narrative authority is grounded. In contrast, Miller suggests, "Austen's divinity is free of all accents that might identify it with a socially accredited broker of power/knowledge in the world under narration. . . . Nowhere else in nineteenth-century English narration have the claims of the 'person,' its ideology, been more completely denied." One of Miller's most striking observations in this essay concerns the extent to which "whoever wishes to illustrate Austen Style regularly gravitates toward the maxim, assuming that the perfection of this Style is highest, most visible and delectable, in bite-size form," even as such maxims are actually relatively uncommon in Austen's fiction; the tendency to extract morsels for anthologies of famous quotations (what Miller calls "the Lilliputian volumes of 'The Wit and Wisdom of Jane Austen' for sale at the counter of certain gift shops") ignores "not just the fact, but the strangeness of the fact, that Austen

Style elects to express itself in, of all things, a *narrative* form" (40–41). The practice of quotation associated with this sort of anthology will *always* distort the sense and workings of the language in the longer narratives from which such quotations are drawn, erasing in particular the tension between the amplitude or unfolding tendencies of narrative and the punctuated or abrupt quality of the aphorism.

I want to invoke an example from Flaubert in order to show this tension at its clearest. "Human speech is like a cracked kettle on which we beat out tunes for bears to dance to, when we long to move the stars to pity": an aphorism, certainly, perhaps even an overextravagant one, almost "unearned" or glib—histrionic to a degree that verges on melodrama—when it is taken as a self-standing unit of prose. Consider it in its context, though, at the end of the passage in *Madame Bovary* that describes the response of Rodolphe to Emma Bovary's expressions of passion:

> He had heard these things said to him so often that for him there was nothing original about them. Emma was like all other mistresses; and the charm of novelty, slipping off gradually like a piece of clothing, revealed in its nakedness the eternal monotony of passion, which always assumes the same forms and uses the same language. He could not perceive—this man of such broad experience—the difference in feelings that might underlie similarities of expression. Because licentious or venal lips had murmured the same words to him, he had little faith in their truthfulness; one had to discount, he thought, exaggerated speeches that concealed mediocre affections; as if the fullness of the soul did not sometimes overflow in the emptiest of metaphors, since none of us can ever express the exact measure of our needs, or our ideas, or our sorrows, and human speech is like

a cracked kettle on which we beat out tunes for bears to dance to, when we long to move the stars to pity.[7]

To my ear, that sentence, which when taken out of context can only be described as *a bit much*, becomes heartbreaking when placed as it is here, as the culmination of a movement from the narrow angle of Rodolphe's thoughts to the broad summing-up vantage-point of the middle of the paragraph. I think here, too, of an aphorism of Friedrich Nietzsche's often uttered by Harold Bloom (it is the epigraph to his 1998 book *Shakespeare: The Invention of the Human*): "That for which we can find words is already dead in our hearts; there is always a kind of contempt in the act of speaking."

It is often worth asking, about moments in prose that display the acoustical elegance and critical force of the aphorism, at whose expense they come. Is a particular aphorism associated with a character's point of view? A narratorial or authorial point of view? The point of view of a real historical author or of an authorial persona like Fielding's? (There is a slight but distinct difference between saying "narratorial" and "authorial"—the authorial persona is very strong in the narration of *Tom Jones*, for instance, whereas *Emma*'s narrator has a distinct voice but could not be identified as an authorial persona as such.) Aphorisms of judgment are everywhere in Austen's fiction, and they are often curiously and conspicuously unlocalized— associated with but not technically linked to the character whose viewpoint we are closest to at the moment of judgment. Sometimes, indeed, there is no character in the vicinity but merely an impersonal narrative pronouncement, as in the account *Emma*'s second chapter provides of Mr. Weston's earlier marriage to a wealthy young woman whose family disinherited her and who thereafter found his income insufficient to her requirements:

It was an unsuitable connection, and did not produce much happiness. Mrs. Weston ought to have found more in it, for she had a husband whose warm heart and sweet temper made him think every thing due to her in return for the great goodness of being in love with him; but though she had one sort of spirit, she had not the best. She had resolution enough to pursue her own will in spite of her brother, but not enough to refrain from unreasonable regrets at that brother's unreasonable anger, nor from missing the luxuries of her former home. They lived beyond their income, but still it was nothing in comparison of Enscombe: she did not cease to love her husband, but she wanted at once to be the wife of Captain Weston, and Miss Churchill of Enscombe. (*Emma*, I.ii, 13)

This is the impersonal narrator's judgment, surely—we don't hear these words as being associated with the "voice" of a particular character, although it may be that the position would have something in common with the judgment of Emma Woodhouse or the Knightley brothers. The tone is perhaps Augustan in its impersonality; this is a narrator comfortable with discriminating between "one sort of spirit" and "the best" sort of spirit, and the Augustan oppositions continue in the next sentence ("enough . . . not enough . . . nor"). There is no triumphant rounding-out at the end of the paragraph here, as one might find in the closing couplets of certain poems by Pope or Swift ("Such Order from Confusion sprung, / Such gaudy Tulips rais'd from Dung"), no verbally resounding clincher, but instead a sort of "sideways" summing-up that flowers out of the word *Enscombe* as a kind of second thought. The words "it is nothing in comparison of Enscombe" may indeed be Mrs. Weston's own, filtered into the third-person narrative by means of free indirect style, which allows the words or thoughts of an individual character to migrate into a free-floating narrative voice that both is and isn't associated with that particular person, but they prompt a ratcheting-up of verbal intensity on the narrator's part, and the final observation about the lady's contradictory desires is calmly devastating.

More often, though, moments of satirical judgment do seem to be linked to an individual character's point of view. It is a striking characteristic of Austen's style, this use of the third-person voice that can home in so closely on a single character's thoughts that we get them seemingly almost unmediated—and yet always necessarily mediated by their frame. Free indirect style (as opposed, on the one hand, to direct speech, and on the other to a close or limited third-person paraphrase that lacks the quality of freedom, that ability to swoop freely in and out on multiple characters' perspectives) is a powerful and flexible tool for the novelist writing in the third person. Such narration is able to zoom in on the thoughts of an individual character and then move back out again with astonishing rapidity and effectiveness. (James Wood, in *How Fiction Works*, gives us a classic example from the opening of Joyce's story "The Dead": "'Lily, the caretaker's daughter, was literally run off her feet.' But no one is *literally* run off her feet."[8]) In Austen's version of the mode, at least, there's also a strong component of judgment or summing-up, the sense that a narrator has selected crucial phrases or sentences from some conjectural conversation to which we don't have direct access but that will represent not just telling details but in many cases damning ones, characters condemned by having the words borrowed out of their own mouths.

In the taxonomy of Austen's style, then, the reporting of a character's thoughts or speech in a third-person voice often exposes that person's foibles. A good instance in *Emma* can be seen in the narrative handling of Mr. Woodhouse's anxieties concerning the disposition of the wedding cake at the end of chapter 2, and the thoughts of Mr. Woodhouse or Mr. Elton or Harriet Smith may come through very strongly and revealingly at individual moments, almost as though the narrative voice is a radio tuned briefly to the channel of one character's thoughts and then to another's. We also see the use of a lightly ironized diction that is not clearly directed toward a specific target. "Not unfrequently, through Emma's persuasion, [Mr. Woodhouse] had some of the chosen and the best to dine with him" (I.iii.17): the double negative of "Not unfrequently" and that phrase "the chosen and the best" both sound lurkingly satirical, but whose judgment is it? Does Emma use the phrase "the chosen and the best" self-mockingly, or is it the narrator's mockery of the smallness of the social circles of Hartfield? These questions can't be answered—yet neither can the sentence be taken as simple denotative description absent all judgment.

Style is itself one of *Emma*'s great topics. Think of the moment when we first hear, about the collection of riddles that Emma is amassing with the help of her submissive new friend, Harriet Smith, that "as Harriet wrote a very pretty hand, it was likely to be an arrangement of the first order, in form as well as quantity" (I.ix.56). This is funny because of word choice: a standard opposition might place quantity on the one hand and quality on the other, and neither form nor quantity is really a good criterion of evaluation for such a collection, properly speaking. Elsewhere, the intellectually feeble Mr. Woodhouse offers a verdict on the smooth and plausible letter written by Frank Churchill on the occasion of his father's remarriage that at first seems to discredit Mr. Woodhouse's judgment but that also obliquely discredits Frank Churchill, too, for precisely the pliancy and prettiness of manner which Mr. Knightley has already criticized in Frank. "It was an exceeding good, pretty letter, and gave Mr. and Mrs. Weston a great deal of pleasure," Mr. Woodhouse observes. "I remember it was written from Weymouth, and dated Sept. 28th—and began, 'My dear Madam,' but I forget how it went on; and it was signed 'F. C. Weston Churchill.'— I remember that perfectly" (I.xi.77). Not, then, a letter of substance—but when Isabella Woodhouse exclaims in response to this description "How very pleasing and proper of him!," it is not just a banality. She responds specifically to Frank's choice to use his father's name when he signs the letter, rather than exclusively the surname of the family into which he has been adopted. It was a common practice at this time for a relatively impoverished family of gentry with surplus sons to offer one of them up, as heir, to another branch of the family with more wealth and no offspring, with the name change often being made a condition of the adoption: Jane Austen's brother Edward was adopted by Austen cousins Thomas and Catherine Knight and changed his name to Edward Austen Knight. It seems as though Mr. Woodhouse, with all his trivializing impulses (his lack of a sense of proportion), has after all singled out the letter's most salient feature.

Many of the sharper insights of *Emma* the novel seem to be at least loosely aligned with the point of view of Emma the character, but this is not always the case—and even when it is, it raises as many questions as it answers. Whose irony is it, for instance, when the narrator proclaims, of the visit from Emma's sister and her family, that "she had nothing to wish otherwise, but that the days did not pass so swiftly. It was a delightful visit;—perfect, in being much too short" (I.xiii.86). "She" is sister Isabella, but the insight that a visit should always be "much too short" cannot derive from Isabella's dim consciousness, and part of the joke—I will spell out the obvious, in a way that leaches out the humor but that lets me draw attention to the mechanics of the sentence—is that even people we like very much become tiresome when they visit us for too long, especially if their children are noisy. If this is Emma's dry aside, though, how does the narrator move so quickly from Isabella's consciousness to that of her sister? Or is it simply the narrator's interjection, as it were, from on high? The same cadence can be heard in a later, better-known line concerning the elaborate preparations for a group visit to Box Hill: "Nothing was wanting but to be happy when they got there" (III.vii.288). This is certainly the *kind* of thing that Emma might think or say, but it is unanchored, unmoored— the novel gives it no unambiguous point of origin in a single character's filtering consciousness.

Here is another, fuller example that even more clearly bares the enigma of the novel's narrative voice. Emma has under-taken the difficult task of breaking the news to Harriet Smith that despite Emma's encouragement to both parties (and par-ticularly to Harriet), Mr. Elton has understood the object of his pursuit to be Emma herself rather than her less-well-off friend. Harriet's "tears fell abundantly," the narrator com-ments (we deduce from the rest of the sentence that this is not much to her credit),

> but her grief was so truly artless, that no dignity could have made it more respectable in Emma's eyes—and she listened to her and tried to console her with all her heart and understanding—really for a time convinced that Harriet was the superior creature of the two—and that to resemble her would be more for her own welfare and happiness than all that genius or intelligence could do.
>
> It was rather too late in the day to set about being simple-minded and ignorant; but she left her with every previous resolution confirmed of being humble and dis-creet, and repressing imagination all the rest of her life. (I.xvii.112)

The modifier "really" is a signal of sincerity—there is nothing sarcastic about Emma's conviction, short-lived though it may be, of Harriet's superiority. But what has happened between the end of that paragraph and the beginning of the next one? "It was rather too late in the day to set about being simple-minded and ignorant"—is the sarcasm Emma's or the narrator's? Surely the ring of the words owes something to the sound of Emma's own unspoken thoughts. The sentence is funny because of the tension between the status of these adjectives as performing a function of simple description and as they fulfill a function of judgment—the comedy arises from the nonmalicious use of judgmental words as though they are simply neutral. The rest of the sentence takes an interesting turn. It absolutely doesn't have the rounded-out cadence of a rhymed couplet; instead, it swerves. There is no irony in Emma's own state of mind at her departure; whatever irony resides in the passage must arise from the narrator's framing and phrasing of the situation. (In that sense, the joke here is surely at Emma's expense rather than being produced by Emma's own consciousness.) The passage, in other words, at once gives voice to Emma's thoughts and offers a place from which they may be held up to judgment or critiqued themselves; it is not, perhaps, an unstable form of irony, but it destabilizes the reader slightly, wrong-footing us a little and putting us off balance.

Another instance in which participation is combined with critique—in which critique is made possible by the act of participatory ventriloquism—appears in a later installment of the subplot in which Emma continually misunderstands the ways in which men respond to Harriet and Harriet to the men around her. By this point in the novel, we have learned to question Emma's own apprehension of events: in light of the earlier failure of Emma's attempt to match-make between Harriet and Mr. Elton, her notion of building on the scene in which Frank Churchill "rescues" Harriet from the gypsies is automatically rendered suspicious. (Indeed, it will emerge that in the conversation Emma has with Harriet about that rescue, they are truly speaking at cross-purposes, Harriet having understood Emma to refer instead to Mr. Knightley's gallant intervention to save her from public embarrassment at a dance.) Suspicion arises in part as a consequence of the hyperbole of the narrative recounting of Emma's position:

> Such an adventure as this,—a fine young man and a lovely young woman thrown together in such a way, could hardly fail of suggesting certain ideas to the coldest heart and the steadiest brain. So Emma thought, at least. Could a linguist, could a grammarian, could even a mathematician have seen what she did, have witnessed their appearance together, and heard their history of it, without feeling that circumstances had been at work to make them peculiarly interesting to each other?—How much more must an imaginist, like herself, be on fire with speculation and foresight!—especially with such a ground-work of anticipation as her mind had already made. (III.iii.263)

Here the fidelity of the words to Emma's own thoughts— the switch may be as little as "she" for "I" and "herself" for "myself," as even the verb tenses would work for a first-person ejaculation, barring the need for the present-tense "have" and "has" rather than "had"—contributes to the effectiveness of Emma's exposure. Rhetorically, we expect these hopes will prove unfounded—their bounce is suspicious—and we are perhaps alerted to that suspicion by the narrator's dry disclaimer in the second sentence ("So Emma thought, at least").

This passage ironically echoes Emma's earlier resolution of "repressing imagination all the rest of her life"; she is irrepressibly an "imaginist" (in the first edition, that unusual noun was capitalized), one who takes speculation to be synonymous with foresight in a consequential misprision whose correction may lead to painful self-castigation later on. The novel enacts a strange dance of punishment and celebration around both imagination and judgment, the practice of each of which, incorrectly grounded in false perception and ethical irresponsibility, may lead to the most penetrating humiliation for the rash practitioner, but which together constitute (when properly practiced) not just the layperson's ordinary obligation but the novelist's peculiar one. I suppose that as a child, I loved *Pride and Prejudice* most out of all Austen's novels because of its fairytale symmetries and precision-tooled language, but each subsequent stage of life has brought me to a new favorite. As an adolescent, I began to identify more strongly with *Sense and Sensibility*, a great novel of emotional disarray and pointed argument, and in graduate school, with the potent abjection of dependent Fanny Price; but in the full adulthood of middle age, I have to confess that *Emma* has become my undoubted favorite among all Austen's novels, partly for its structural and narrative subtleties but also because of its commitment to depicting the costs of well-intentioned meddling on behalf of others. As professors, we too often believe in our own ability to discern and our right to determine the fates of others, and *Emma* tells a story about the outcomes we try to impose on others that seems to me at least as cautionary as Daniel Kahneman's revelations about the shortcomings of common decision-making protocols in *Thinking, Fast and Slow*.

5

Tempo, Repetition and a Taxonomy of Pacing

Peter Temple, Neil Gaiman, A. L. Kennedy, Edward P. Jones

A passage of prose experienced on the page doesn't exist as obviously in time as a snatch of music or a theatrical scene. That doesn't mean time doesn't matter when we're reading. A number of the most striking verbal effects depend on the temporal dimension. Pace constitutes an important and sometimes neglected element of storytelling (we're probably more aware of it in TV writing than in narrative fiction, due to the historical impact of tight temporal constraints in network television); the speed at which we read something is not supposed to affect the reading experience in any deep way, but I suspect that reading *War and Peace* feels significantly different when it is completed in ten hours versus in a hundred, and TV and film are in that sense more democratic than novels, insofar as they impose a uniform pace of consumption across the entire audience. The massive scale of a *Clarissa* or an *In Search of Lost Time* makes even a fast reader experience the book as a world to be entered rather than a story to be consumed, and a sense of dilation, of almost unutterably prolonged immersion, is crucial to the effects that each of those novels produces.

On a smaller scale, the stylistic impact of verbal repetition also depends on the fact that words exist in time. Henry Watson Fowler, in his 1926 dictionary of usage, urged the reader to avoid what he called "elegant variation" and deplored the "fatal influence" of "the advice given to young writers never to use the same word twice in a sentence." Elegant variation can of course be turned to very good ends—the effulgence of a baroque sensibility, the instrument of a comedy of self-aggrandizement and self-deflation. It should never be ruled out automatically, and it's this sort of dictum ("Omit needless words") that similarly gives Strunk and White a bad name in certain circles. That said, concision is a useful guideline for inexperienced writers; indeed, the willful repetition of a single word can produce desirable effects well beyond the point at which most writers would lose their nerve and reach for the synonym. Here is a favorite passage from one of my very favorite writers, Peter Temple:

Against the righthand wall were the clamp racks: at the bottom, the monster sash clamps; above them, the lesser sizes; in the next rack, the bar clamps, the infantry of joinery, dozens of them in every size; then the frame clamps, the spring clamps, the G-clamps, the ancient wooden screw clamps that Charlie loved best, and flexible wooden go-bars arranged by length. Finally, an assortment of weird clamps, many of them invented by Charlie to solve particular clamping problems.[1]

The rubric "clamp racks" introduces an amazing array of clamps, the verbal momentum building up to the final catch-all category of "weird clamps" and their application to "clamping problems," with the unexpected transformation of the noun into the adjectival form "clamping" providing a conclusion that feels strangely provisional, off-kilter, unsettled. Temple's novels are published as crime fiction, which is probably the genre most hospitable to a stringent and beautiful ideal of prose in the tradition of Beckett (I think of practitioners like Derek Raymond and Ken Bruen). In his most recent books, Temple has perfected an idiom that is on the one hand estranging or defamiliarizing and on the other still appealingly and effectively load-bearing in the narrative sense. Crime fiction tends to feature stronger plots than literary fiction, and it also often carries a sociological freight as a result of its desire to portray broken societies and explore the problem of human evil.[2] But Temple's use of, say, the hyphen greatly exceeds the matter-of-fact needs of sentence-writing in popular fiction, as this sentence from his 2005 novel *The Broken Shore* shows: "The vinegary couple from the newsagency were in their shop doorway, mouths curving southwards. Triple-bypassed Bruce of the video shop was beside saturated-fat dealer Meryl, the fish and chip shop owner."[3] Satire lurks in the descriptive language as well as in the physical juxtaposition of victim and pusher of saturated fats, and the distinctive effect here is one of compression; the easy conventions of English word order are snubbed, as is the common injunction to avoid using conjugations of the verb "to be" in favor of active verbs.

While there's something humorous about Temple's clamp passage, comedy isn't the primary verbal effect of the repetition. In other hands, though, that sort of repetition can be extremely funny in a way that calls to mind the routines of *The Goon Show* or Monty Python's famous "Spam" sketch but that's probably as old as Aristophanes. (Or even older—it seems to me that verbal repetition works on the basis of something fundamental about language and cognition rather than being a literary innovation anchored in one writer's imagination at some specific location in time and space.) Influenced by the tradition of verbal sketch comedy (the *Blackadder* scripts also come to mind), British novelists like Terry Pratchett and Neil Gaiman have made themselves masters of repetition as a comic effect. This kind of joke works not just by lavish repetition but also by subverting the proper forms of similes and metaphors so that they fold back in on themselves. The pace of Gaiman's novel *Anansi Boys*, for instance, is quite gentle, definitely not uproarious, so that the periodic outright comedy catches the reader slightly off guard:

> It was sort of like *Macbeth*, thought Fat Charlie, an hour later; in fact, if the witches in *Macbeth* had been four little old ladies, and if instead of stirring cauldrons and intoning dread incantations they had just welcomed Macbeth in and fed him on turkey, and rice and peas, spread out on white china plates on a red-and-white patterned plastic table cloth, not to mention sweet potato pudding and spicy cabbage, and encouraged him to take second helpings, and thirds, and then, when Macbeth had declaimed that nay, he was stuffed nigh unto bursting and on his oath could truly eat no more, the witches had pressed upon him their own special island rice pudding and a large slice of Mrs Bustamonte's famous pineapple upside-down cake, it would have been exactly like *Macbeth*.[4]

This passage derives its energy from the comic contrast between the Shakespearean high-cultural reference (the bits of Jacobean pastiche) and the everyday familiarity of the four little ladies cooking up a Caribbean meal; the name Macbeth is used five times in a single sentence, structuring and elevating the cadence even as the naming of rice pudding and pineapple upside-down cake serves to deflate. The next example foregrounds two separate acts of verbal repetition. Spider, impersonating his brother Fat Charlie, creates an illusion of that identity simply by asserting it:

> "I'm Fat Charlie Nancy," said Spider.
> "Why is he saying that?" asked Rosie's mother. "Who is he?"
> "I'm Fat Charlie Nancy, your future son-in-law, and you really like me," said Spider, with utter conviction.
> Rosie's mother swayed and blinked and stared at him.
> "You may be Fat Charlie," she said uncertainly, "but I don't like you."
> "Well," said Spider, "you should. I am remarkably likeable. Few people have ever been as likeable as I am. There is, frankly, no end to my likeability. People gather together in public assemblies to discuss how much they like me. I have several awards, and a medal from a small country in South America which pays tribute both to how much I am liked and my general all-around wonderfulness. I don't have it on me, of course. I keep my medals in my sock drawer." (162)

Magic works in this book by way of language, not as a function of arcane systems of learning, so that Spider's playful but purposeful elaboration of the notion that his mother-in-law-to-be really likes him is the way he makes it so: "likeable," "likeable," "likeability," and then the transition back through the verbal forms ("how much they like me," "how much I am liked") into the more expansive assertion of "my general all-round wonderfulness" and the deflationary self-deprecation of the explanation that the medals are stashed in his sock drawer. The last example I will give from Gaiman's novel is a bit simpler than the other two, and for that reason reveals even more clearly the way the humor works: "The world was his lobster, his bib was round his neck, and he had a pot of melted butter and an array of grotesque but effective lobster-eating implements and devices at the ready" (175). It's the repetition of the word "lobster," stuck into the phrase "an array of grotesque but effective lobster-eating implements," that I find charming, though I can also see how a reader might find it annoying or overly whimsical.

Repetition can be comic, but it can also be surreal. Luc Sante offers an interesting analysis of the dummy placeholder word and the ways it can invoke the uncanny in his discussion of the best-known characters of *Spirou*, the French-language comic magazine he grew up reading, "Les Schtroumpfs, known in the English-speaking world as the Smurfs, small blue elfin creatures who lived in a toadstool village":

In their English-language animated appearances they could be cloyingly cute, but in French they were spared this fate by their language, marked by an incessant use of the (invented) word *schtroumpf*, employed as noun, verb, adverb, adjective, and interjection. Every reader, no matter how young, understood this usage without a gloss, because it parodied the French conversational trope of substituting catch-alls such as *truc*, *chose*, and *machin* for words that cannot immediately be called to mind, in any grammatical position. What *schtroumpf* highlighted was the ability of such dummy words to suggest words prohibited from writing or speech, regardless of the fact that the actual words *schtroumpf* was substituting for were always clear from context. *Truc* or *chose* became neutral from exposure, but *schtroumpf* subliminally spoke to the unconscious; its surface strangeness could make it mean things that the child's mind does not yet know but can imagine with tantalizing vagueness.[5]

I don't think English speakers have a comparably strong habit of catch-all substitution, though it might be that an obscenity like *mother-fucker* does some of the same work in certain speakers' idiolects. (One of the strangest and most characteristic features of Chester Himes's crime fiction derives from his use of the euphemism "mother-raper" in place of the then-unprintable "mother-fucker," and his contemporaries fell back on terms like "mother-jumper" and "mother-fouler" for the same reason.)[6] Inherently uncanny is the fact that the human mind has such a strong grasp on meaning that even a sentence missing all of its proper nouns can be readily understood, the estranging joke made by Sterne by way of the ellipses of *Tristram Shandy*: "The chamber maid had left no ******* *** under the bed:—cannot you contrive, master, quoth *Susannah*, lifting up the sash with one hand, as she spoke, and helping me up into the window seat with the other,—Cannot you manage, my dear, for a single time to **** *** ** *** ******?"[7] A debate roiled during the period in which that novel was written as to whether pregnant women might rely more properly and prudently on female midwives or male physicians; Mrs. Shandy prefers the local midwife to Dr. Slop, a preference Uncle Toby accounts for very bluntly: "My sister, I dare say, added he, does not care to let a man come so near her ****" (*Tristram Shandy*, II.vi.89). The asterisks are four, the word is "arse," and Tristram repeats his uncle's words and ruminates upon them:

Make this dash,——'tis an Aposiopesis.—Take the dash away, and write Backside,—'tis Bawdy.—Scratch Backside out, and put *Cover'd-way* in,—'tis a Metaphor;—and, I dare say, as fortification ran so much in my uncle *Toby*'s head, that if he had been left to have added one word to the sentence,—that word was it.

Any given novel can be thought of as having its own pace or set of paces; some writers pace very consistently both within and across novels (this is obviously true for a great deal of genre fiction—let's say the thrillers of Lee Child or the science fiction novels of Iain M. Banks—but it could also be said of Anne Tyler or Paulo Coelho), while others write books of more variable pacing (Kate Christensen's *Trouble*, Ed Park's *Personal Days*) or seem to vary their pacing deliberately from one book to the next (*Motherless Brooklyn* versus *The Fortress of Solitude*). Neil Gaiman's novels are striking for their very marked differences in terms of structure and pacing, from the fantastic baggy monster of *American Gods*—which seems to contain several different novels within its multitudes—to the fable-like economy of *Stardust* or the Kiplingesque cumulative tale-compilation of *The Graveyard Book*. The prose of novels often differs from the prose of short stories partly because of some real though hard-to-pin-down aspects of pacing, momentum and directionality, none of which are things that literary-critical terminology is especially well equipped to deal with. The following passage seems to me a good example not just of alluring prose but of prose that, while it is beautifully "crafted" in a way I associate with the literary short story, can also be said to display the rhythms of full-length novel pacing. It is from A. L. Kennedy's *Paradise*:

You are now approaching forty and have already spent far too long washing underwear in a theatre, stacking shelves, cleaning rental power tools—which are, I would mention, often returned in revolting states. You have slotted together grids of doubtful purpose, you have

folded free knitting and/or sewing patterns into wom-
en's magazines, you have sorted potatoes (for three grotesque hours), you have telephoned telephone owners to
tell them about their telephones and you have spent one
extremely long weekend in a hotel conference suite, asking people what they found most pleasing about bags
of crisps. Every prior experience proves it—there is no
point to you.

At least at the end of the crisps job, I got to take some
home. But selling cardboard was a godsend: flexible and
satisfying in a way that involved no pressure at any stage,
because—after all—what sane person could possibly
care about who might be buying how many of which
kind of box. The job actually managed to be more trivial
than me, which seemed to produce this Zen glow across
my better days and enabled me to lie my head off in a
consistent, promotional manner with hardly a trace of
nauseous side effects.

At the moment, though, there's nothing doing: not in
cardboard. Nobody wants me any more and yet, for the
usual reasons, I continue to want cash. So, on a sodden
Tuesday lunchtime, I'm forced to admit I've been driven
to make the drinker's most conventional mistake. I've
started working in a bar.[8]

The second-person address "you" is self-consciously literary (the best-known example of second-person narration
is probably Jay McInerney's *Bright Lights, Big City*, and it
always gives a slight "stunt writing" feel), but the narrator
reverts to the plainer "I" after that initial list-like compila-
tion of job histories (this passage falls a good way into the
novel as a whole). There are funny moments, including ones
produced by that trick of repetition ("you have telephoned
telephone owners to tell them about their telephones"), but

the overall effect is relentlessly self-denigrating. The *time* of narration is also unusually slippery here: second-person continuous present-tense address in paragraph one, then a switch into the more straightforward first-person past tense in paragraph two before the disorienting leap of paragraph three, which omits the actual transition from past to present and plunges into the present tense of the current job on a Tuesday lunchtime when alcohol has already been consumed. The last paragraph is clearly going to work as a sort of hinge or joint: there is movement; the next stretch of narration will be attached to this bit and will strike out in a different direction. When I say that the next stretch will exist sideways to the previous one, I have in mind the contrast with a different form of narration in which the story feels less like a vector and more like a structure or model, with each piece functioning as a particular brick might serve in stabilizing an arch, set in the one inevitable place it can possibly belong. That is the feeling that many very good short stories give: it is not the only way a short story can be paced, but it is the kind of pacing that makes the stories of Nathan Englander or Yiyun Li attractive to me despite my general preference for longer fiction.

I have a lurking feeling that I have not yet persuasively made my case about how pacing works in short stories versus the novel, so I want to give two simpler examples that will perhaps clarify the point. I was very struck, some years ago, by the richness of style in evidence in the sentences of this extract from a diary Tobias Hill kept during his stint as a writer-in-residence at Eton. Here Hill has inadvertently allowed a pan of milk to boil over in the suite where he's staying:

There is nothing seductive about the lactic mire of the electric oven. The Hodgson Guest Suite is indeed roomy, but it is cavernous and utilitarian, everything foursquare and scrubbed to the quick. "All the mod cons" is an estate agent's way of putting it, too: all cons are present, but the mod is that of a bygone decade. Vinyl seats, flaked white goods, ironing board (though maybe all normal people have ironing boards; maybe it's just crumpled writers who don't). Marmoleum.[9]

"The lactic mire of the electric oven": I like the phrase, it catches my eye, and yet I feel it's the kind of stylistic flourish that detracts from the effectiveness of the prose as a whole. The diction is appealing, and yet there's also something a little purposeless or show-offy, it doesn't ring quite true: what is this passage *for*? It is unfair, perhaps, to complain of a diary entry's seeming undermotivated; it is a perfectly reasonable practice of the genre to offer description for its own sake, and there is no expectation that a diary entry should have the momentum or propulsion of a short story or essay (nor yet the punch of a deliberately composed aphorism). But I can't shake the feeling that the style is insufficiently called forth by the occasion; this may be related to the kinds of insecurity Hill attributes to himself earlier in the piece (he is the product of comprehensive education rather than public schooling, making Eton a potentially stressful environment), as if he exerts himself to produce these verbal flourishes partly out of a rush of social-educational anxiety, of thinking a little too much about how or what he's supposed to be thinking.

In contrast to this passage which I have called undermotivated, I would instance a thematically similar extract from a short story by William Boyd, "The Things I Stole" (it is definitely presented as fiction, and I have no reason to believe it isn't entirely "made up," but the first-person narrator is rendered in a plausible and low-key fashion that gives the story the feel of a nonfictional personal essay):

I stole food at my boarding school. We were allowed a modest food parcel once a week (like POWs) from a local grocer: a few bananas, a box of dates, mini-packs of cornflakes—no buns or cakes, no chocolates, nothing that could be purchased from the school tuck shop where fizzy drinks, colas, biscuits and every tooth-rotting sweet the confectionery industry could serve up were on offer.

In my house there was a very rich Greek boy whose food parcel might have come from Fortnum & Mason, such was its size and magnificence. I and my coevals pillaged this boy's food with no compunction (he was plump and cried easily). It was thanks to Stavros's food parcel that I developed my enduring taste for Patum Peperium, Gentleman's Relish, a dark, pesto-like spread made from anchovies. It is my Proustian madeleine—it summons up all my early pilfering. I can taste its earthy, farinaceous salinity now.[10]

This falls somewhere between Hill's diary entry and Kennedy's novel. It is "motivated" or purposeful in a way that Hill's extract isn't. But it doesn't have the hinge-like quality of the passage from Kennedy's novel either; there is movement of a kind (the last line I quote uses the tongue's sense of taste to bring the past alive in the present), but the tact of the pacing feels to me more characteristic of short story than novel. We sense this to be a satisfactory little chunk of a construction that will probably, once we have read it in its entirety, give the feel of structural self-sufficiency; we don't imagine that we are likely to be pointed in a wholly unexpected new direction.

One of the most unusual relationships to time in narration that I have ever encountered can be found in the fictions of Edward P. Jones, a writer for whom I feel an admiration mounting almost to idolatry. He has published only one novel, and that book shares many features with the short stories he has been composing over a much more extended period. His effects seem to work equally well in long and short forms, unlike, say, Yiyun Li, whose stories I find exquisite and memorable but whose novel *The Vagrants* lacked that sense of formal perfection and inevitability and didn't offer anything that seemed sufficient compensation for their absence. When I reviewed his collection *All Aunt Hagar's Children* for the *Voice Literary Supplement* in 2006, I could only say that Jones "writes as God might, were He to publish fiction": he mobilizes a relatively unusual verb tense to embed the future in the past, and every single incident in his characters' lives is simultaneously present to the stories' omniscient narrator (who is also in this sense a kind of celestial census taker).[11] The property called Patches' Creek belongs to a woman who "fancied herself the richest Negro in Mississippi" but "would die not knowing there were five undertakers and one insurance company founder who were richer"; the battered but intact female protagonist of "Common Law" is "one and a half years from marrying Alvin Deloach," "more than eight years from marrying Vaughn Anderson," "just about thirty years from seeing her first grandchild come into the world," and "more than forty and a half years from death."[12] With this orientation, Jones diverts the reader's attention almost entirely away from the question of what will happen, a curious and moving technique unmatched elsewhere in contemporary fiction. It speaks to the sweeping aspirations of the realist novel that God's notional omniscience should be the implicit model for talking about the narrative voice of *Tom Jones* or *Middlemarch*, but even omniscient narration in the novel is tied down to a specific temporal vantage point, and to a unidirectional flow of time from past to present; Jones transcends that limitation more fully than any other writer I can think of.

6

Late Style

The Golden Bowl and *Swann's Way*

We develop unevenly as readers. I remember feeling furious, at age fifteen, when the father of one of my brothers' friends (a psychology professor at Temple) questioned my
ability to understand the novels of Dostoevsky. It was not that
he doubted my cognitive capacities; rather, he didn't credit me
with the emotional experience and maturity to really comprehend the matters with which Dostoevsky is concerned. I
thought he was wrong then, and I still think he's wrong now,
though for somewhat different reasons. It is my observation
that the novels of Dostoevsky (and, for different reasons, of
Tolstoy as well) are peculiarly suited to the emotional and intellectual range of teenagers. The novels celebrate raw painful
forms of emotion and emotionally intense forms of political
and religious commitment that will resonate very fully with

people between the ages of sixteen and nineteen. Of course, not all books open themselves up so readily at that stage of life. I remember reading two essays by Hume (one of them must have been "Of the Original Contract") for Judith Shklar's lecture course on political obligation, at age twenty or so, and finding them obscure, opaque, dare I say *boring* compared to the more obviously literary works on the syllabus (*Richard II*, Heinrich von Kleist's *Prince Friedrich of Homburg*, *Murder In the Cathedral*); three years later, with a much fuller knowledge of seventeenth- and eighteenth-century political thought, the same essays had become extraordinarily lucid, not just comprehensible but magically clear, as clear and easy to read as I had found Orwell's essays at sixteen. It was as though someone had pulled a trick on me and switched the texts: I could have sworn I was reading an altogether different sequence of words this time around.

There is something to be said for waiting to read a given book until one is truly prepared to plunge into its depths. I read *Moby-Dick* on my own, the summer after my first year of graduate school (a year in which the book that most struck me with the force of revelation was *Paradise Lost*, which, strange to say, I had never read before); I had previously avoided Herman Melville's novel on the mistaken belief that it was a sea story along tedious and vaguely Conradian lines. (I have always been immune to Joseph Conrad's charms, though I make an exception for *The Secret Agent*, which, along with Dostoevsky's *Demons* and James's *The Princess Casamassima*, seems to me to capture perfectly the ways in which the later decades of the nineteenth century eerily anticipate the romance of terror in the first decade of the twenty-first.) Nothing could have been further from the truth: like the opening books of *Paradise Lost*, *Moby-Dick* is electrifyingly strange, mesmerizing, lovely (I now saw where Pynchon had gotten so many of his effects). I loved *Moby-Dick* so much that part of me was angry that nobody had told me sooner how genuinely great it was, great in the colloquial sense rather than the canonical one, although it might be that if I'd encountered it sooner, I wouldn't have been so well primed to fall in love with it.

It is George Eliot and Henry James, I think, out of all the great canonical English-language novelists, who are better read in one's twenties or beyond rather than in one's teens. I remember reading *Middlemarch* the summer I turned sixteen and finding it worthwhile but very slightly tedious for reasons that had nothing to do with length: I had devoured *Bleak House* almost in a single sitting a few years earlier and would drink down *War and Peace* over a few addictive days two summers later, but *Middlemarch* felt sticky, slow, ponderous. The same thing goes, only even more so, for *The Ambassadors* and *The Golden Bowl*. The German critic Theodor Adorno, writing of Beethoven's late style, observed, "The maturity of the late works of significant artists does not resemble the kind one finds in fruit. They are, for the most part, not round, but furrowed, even ravaged. Devoid of sweetness, bitter and spiny, they do not surrender themselves to mere delectation. They lack all the harmony that the classicist aesthetic is in the habit of demanding from works of art, and they show more traces of history than of growth."[1] Like Beethoven, Henry James is often said to have a "late" style: a way of writing sentences that would become increasingly baroque to the point of being sometimes bizarre, laying bare the conventions that governed his earlier works in a fashion that renders the late novels deeply strange. Part of that transformation is attributed to James's adoption, late in his career, of dictation as his main mode of composition, a practice that allowed his sentences to spiral into ever-more-intricate constructions whose complexity is more readily parsed by eye than ear but that owes much to a cognitive dimension opened up by means of the speaking voice. His biographer, Leon Edel, notes that the sound of the spoken voice is very strong in James's later manner, "not only in the rhythm and ultimate perfection of his verbal music, but in his use of colloquialisms, and in a greater indulgence in metaphor."[2]

First published in 1904, *The Golden Bowl* was James's last major novel, and its sentences display a virtually unprecedented subtlety and complexity, indeed to a degree that many readers have found maddening. James performed extensive revisions on the typescripts of his novels, including a massive wholesale rewriting of his entire oeuvre for publication in the famous New York Edition: an authoritative, multivolume edition of his own fiction. He wrote a preface for the republication of *The Golden Bowl* in that edition that gives some clues as to his concerns, and I will single out two particular points from it before plunging into the thickets of the novel itself for what it shows about how language mediates perception and what possibilities exist for the notation of various forms of cognition in sentences and paragraphs. I should warn the reader in advance that partly because I follow James's difficult novel closely, and perhaps for other reasons as well, this chapter is probably the hardest to read in the entire book, and it will not represent a failure of spirit on the reader's part to skip ahead to the next one.

First of all, James notes in the book "the still marked inveteracy of a certain indirect and oblique view of my presented action."[3] By "inveteracy," James refers to a trait that is ingrained or deep-rooted, habitual, and the unusual word choice is highly characteristic of his style more generally, as is the hint of archness in the locution "a certain. . . ." Amplifying this point further, James observes that he prefers to see the incidents of a story "through the opportunity and the sensibility of some more or less detached, some not strictly involved, though thoroughly interested and intelligent, witness or reporter, some person who contributes to the case mainly a certain amount of criticism and interpretation of it." Again, the syntax is highly rhetorical, the tag *some* giving the sentence energy as the verbal momentum builds, then repeated to give the sentence a second kick after it has built to the nouns *witness* and *reporter*; the term *case*, too, suggests that there is something forensic or medical about the story. Another way of describing this habit, some lines further on, is to say that the novel "remains subject to the register, ever so closely kept, of the consciousness of but two of the characters" (4): register is a noun here, of course, implying the sort of record maintained by a shopkeeper or any other kind of chronicler or historian, but its use in this context brings with it the echo of the associated verb, in which we "register" things precisely because they come into our consciousness. Thus we can see a sort of "working backward," in which James tugs "register" back from its metaphorical usage as a relatively common verb to its root meaning as a noun, thereby showing us something new about the very language we use to pin down and conceptualize the phenomena of perception.

The other point I want to mention from the novel's preface concerns the relationship between written and spoken language, language taken in through the eye versus the ear. In one sense, James can be thought of as a highly *writerly* literary stylist, one whose sentences may be more effectively decoded by the powerful eye than by the emotionally sharp but less cognitively acute ear (at least it is commonly conceived to be so). James, though, explodes that distinction as nonsensical, despite the fact that the language he uses to make the point would present to most auditors a challenge beyond comprehension (even the sharpest-eyed reader may need to move the eyes several times over some of the phrases here—"*viva-voce*," by the way, simply means "by mouth" or "by word of mouth," and is also used in the British educational system to describe what Americans would more likely call an oral exam):

It is scarce necessary to note that the highest test of any literary form conceived in the light of "poetry"— to apply that term in its largest literary sense—hangs back unpardonably from its office when it fails to lend itself to *viva-voce* treatment. We talk here, naturally, not of non-poetic forms, but of those whose highest bid is addressed to the imagination, to the spiritual and the aesthetic vision, the mind led captive by a charm and a spell, an incalculable art. The essential property of such a form as that is to give out its finest and most numerous secrets, and to give them out most gratefully, under the closest pressure—which is of course the pressure of the attention articulately *sounded*. (20)

James likes the trick of apposition, joining by a comma two words or phrases that are thus deemed equivalent ("the mind led captive by a charm and a spell, an incalculable art") even as the exact nature of the equivalence cannot be specified. Sounded, these sentences do not soar in the elegant, unclotted forms associated with elocution or classical rhetoric; they wind back upon themselves, making what is open secret and vice versa.

The Golden Bowl is full of objects: the American father and daughter, Adam and Maggie Verver, who are two of the novel's four main characters (the other two are the Prince, whom Maggie will marry, and Charlotte Stant, who will marry Adam), are in Europe to purchase beautiful objects for the American museum Adam has made his monument, and the novel's title immediately directs our attention to the artifact that will become the instrument of knowledge and revenge. The episode in which the golden bowl is initially discovered represents the culmination of the novel's first book. It is a condensed and telling scene in which Charlotte and the Prince (the pair of whom Fanny Assingham has wishfully asserted, to her curious husband, that "nothing" has taken place between them, "except their having to recognize that nothing *could*" [76]) converse intimately in a highly idiomatic Italian that they assume gives them absolute privacy but that turns out to be fully comprehensible to the antique shop's owner.

The Prince, indeed, has himself been described by Maggie at one point as a "*morceau de musée*" (33), and the boundaries between objects and people are as often blurred as those between objects and verbal metaphors. Charles Sainte-Beuve criticized Flaubert for itemizing the different parts of a woman's appearance so as to blind the reader to her totality rather than help him apprehend it, and James does something rather similar in a curiously nonrealistic or nonnaturalistic mode of representation. Here are the sentences in which Charlotte Stant is described upon her first appearance (the narration is in the third person, but the character who provides the lens through which she is viewed is the Prince himself):

> Making use then of clumsy terms of excess, the face was too narrow and too long, the eyes not large, and the mouth on the other hand by no means small, with substance in its lips and a slight, the very slightest, tendency to protrusion in the solid teeth, otherwise indeed well arrayed and flashingly white. But it was, strangely, as a cluster of possessions of his own that these things in Charlotte Stant now affected him; items in a full list, items recognized, each of them, as if, for the long interval, they had been "stored"—wrapped up, numbered, put away in a cabinet. (58)

Where does the marking "stored" come from? Is it the Prince's emphasis or the narrator's? Or could it be more usefully thought of as the narrator's visual registering, on the page, of something marked in the unspoken language of the Prince's thoughts? It seems to be a habit of the narrator's to mark words in this way, calling to mind Susan Sontag's "Notes on 'Camp'" ("Style sees everything in quotation marks").[4]

I ask the question not to invite a definite answer but rather to direct the attention to this odd feature of James's style. The itemization of the parts of a beautiful woman's face inevitably recalls the Renaissance trope of the *blason*, though that is at odds with the clinical quality of James's prose (consider the singling-out of the tendency to protrusion in the flashingly white teeth). Beyond that, the passage's central metaphor can be said to display a curiously shimmering aspect. It is rendered unstable by the ambiguity surrounding the question of whether these items exist in a list or in a cabinet, i.e. whether they are to be thought of primarily as written words on a piece of paper or curios stored in the drawers of a piece of furniture. The marked word "stored" does some special work here, or rather the quotation marks let the word work as a hinge between items as items-on-a-list and items as actual physical artifacts. Of course, both are metaphors, but by the time we have become embroiled in all of this business, we are inside rather than outside, thinking rather than looking.

Questions of language are constantly foregrounded. The Prince, his consciousness one of only two that filter events for the reader, has been told that he speaks English too well, and whatever that means exactly, the excellence of his English is such that he finds the language "convenient, oddly, even for his relation with himself" (29). This is convenient for James as well, of course—a coincidence of interests to which the novelist perhaps gestures with that coy modifier "oddly," but the attention to the linguistic texture of human thought is unusual and striking. We are constantly asked to attend, for instance, to the artifice of systems of notation: in the secluded country garden where Maggie and Adam Verver converse together, there is a door with "a slab with a date set above it, 1713, but in the old multiplied lettering" (142), the detail about Roman numerals reminding us by extension that the system of alphabetic transcription is also merely a convention. When the Ververs settle, shortly thereafter, on a bench, the narrator continues: "They knew the bench; it was 'sequestered'—they had praised it for that together before and liked the word." The word *sequestered* has migrated from the Ververs' consciousness—their self-conscious consciousness—into the narration, the borrowing marked by the quotation marks and lingered upon in the narrator's singling-out of the characters' fondness for the word. The boundary between the language of narration and the language of each character's internal consciousness has been rendered highly permeable, with the vocabulary and registers of the narrator regularly sliding into those of characters and vice versa.

Consider this description of Bob Assingham, who "could deal with things perfectly, for all his needs, without getting near them":

This was the way he dealt with his wife, a large proportion of whose meanings he knew he could neglect. He edited for their general economy the play of her mind, just as he edited, savingly, with the stump of a pencil, her redundant telegrams. The thing in the world that was least of a mystery to him was his Club, which he was accepted as perhaps too completely managing, and which he managed on lines of perfect penetration. His connexion with it was really a masterpiece of editing. (74)

Fanny's meanings, in their copiousness (the slide between singular "play" and plural "telegrams" is almost a solecism), are a gabby and hyperbolic text to be pruned by Bob's stringent pencil: the stumpiness of the pencil is a sign of his frugality, as is his insistence on keeping telegrams short in an era when such communications were paid for by the word. Fanny and Bob's conversations are replete with the presence of things not said. James's characters sometimes talk about things one should not talk about, but they also refuse to say what one might think *should* be said, and the prose is often driven by the force of this tension between euphemism (periphrasis, beating about the bush) and the explicit.

More generally, though, the novel provides an extraordinarily elaborate language for talking about knowledge: Charlotte and the Prince, contemplating the Ververs, conclude that this father-and-daughter duo "knew . . . absolutely nothing on earth worth speaking of . . . and they would perhaps sometimes be a little less trying if they would only once for all peacefully admit that knowledge wasn't one of their needs and that they were in fact constitutionally inaccessible to it" (271). The Ververs are holy innocents, the Prince and Charlotte are sullied by experience, the novel retells the story of the Fall: its true subject is the vicious game played first by the experienced with the innocent and then, as the tables are turned, by the innocent with the experienced. It is Maggie who precipitates her father's decision to marry, once she explains how her own marriage to the Prince has rendered Adam Verver vulnerable to the husband-seekers formerly dispelled by Maggie's presence at his side: "It was as if you couldn't be in the market when you were married to *me*. Or rather as if I kept people off, innocently, by being married to you. Now that I'm married to some one else you're, as in consequence, married to nobody. Therefore you may be married to anybody, to everybody. People don't see why you shouldn't be married to *them*" (151). The language used to describe this psychosocial subtlety is involuted indeed, as Adam Verver realizes (the narrator here closely follows Adam's thoughts):

They had made vacant by their marriage his immedi-
ate foreground, his personal precinct—they being the
Princess and the Prince. They had made room in it
for others—so others had become aware. He became
aware himself, for that matter, during the minute Maggie stood there before speaking; and with the sense
moreover of what he saw her see he had the sense of
what she saw *him*. This last, it may be added, would
have been his intensest perception hadn't there the next
instant been more for him in Fanny Assingham. Her
face couldn't keep it from him; she had seen, on top
of everything, in her quick way, what they both were
seeing. (138)

This sentence marks the end of the chapter and also displays many of the traits that James's contemporaries found
tiresome or even ludicrous in his prose style (Max Beerbohm
wrote a very good parody of the late James style in a little
piece called "The Mote in the Middle Distance," and there
are countless other parodies—James must be one of the most
immediately recognizable sentence-writers in the history of
the English language). But James is hardly unaware of the
outrageous nature of what he's doing here, and the next
chapter opens with a wonderful defense of the choices he's
just made:

So much mute communication was doubtless all this
time marvellous, and we may confess to having perhaps
read into the scene prematurely a critical character that
took longer to develop. Yet the quiet hour of reunion
enjoyed that afternoon by the father and the daughter
did really little else than deal with the elements definitely
presented to each in the vibration produced by the return
of the church-goers. (139)

This sort of signal of self-awareness, often consequent upon a particularly extravagant or baroque gesture, can be seen throughout: "The little crisis was of a shorter duration than our account of it," observes the narrator after a scene especially fraught with exchanged glances and words unspoken (60).

Also striking in this novel is the tendency to render material the ineffable processes of human perception (James's brother William was one of the pioneers of empiricist psychology, the teacher of Gertrude Stein, among others, and the person whose work popularized the notion of the "stream of consciousness"). Look at the metaphor James uses here, and the persistence with which the passage sticks with it (it would perhaps be more conventional to retreat from the image to the lived reality, but that doesn't happen):

> Fanny Assingham had at this moment the sense as of a large heaped dish presented to her intelligence and inviting it to a feast—so thick were the notes of intention in this remarkable speech. But she also felt that to plunge at random, to help herself too freely, would—apart from there not being at such a moment time for it—tend to jostle the ministering hand, confound the array and, more vulgarly speaking, make a mess. She picked out after consideration a solitary plum. (215)

"The sense as of": the whole image here is oblique, metaphorical, secondary. But even in the third sentence a "plum" can still be picked out, a plum wholly imaginary but given strange solidity (it is almost caloric) by the act of naming. (The consonant combination "pl" is itself acutely sensory, even aside from the scent and chewiness and color associated with the fruit; it is probably something more like a prune, a date or a raisin than the fragrant fresh fruit—a sugarplum.) Here is another of these extravagantly sustained metaphors (it is impossible to convey their workings without quoting at length):

> [Fanny] felt now that she wouldn't have interrupted [the Prince] for the world. She found his eloquence precious; there wasn't a drop of it that she didn't in a manner catch, as it came, for immediate bottling, for future preservation. The crystal flask of her innermost attention really received it on the spot, and she had even already the vision of how, in the snug laboratory of her afterthought, she should be able chemically to analyse it. There were moments positively, still beyond this, when, with the meeting of their eyes, something as yet unnameable came out for her in his look, when something strange and subtle and at variance with his words, something that *gave them away*, glimmered deep down, as an appeal, almost an incredible one, to her finer comprehension. What, inconceivably, was it like? Wasn't it, however gross such a rendering of anything so occult, fairly like a quintessential wink, a hint of the possibility of their *really* treating their subject—of course on some better occasion—and thereby, as well, finding it much more interesting? If this far red spark, which might have been figured by her mind as the head-light of an approaching train seen through the length of a tunnel, was not, on her side, an *ignis fatuus*, a mere subjective phenomenon, it twinkled there at the direct expense of what the Prince was inviting her to understand. Meanwhile too, however, and unmistakeably, the real treatment of their subject did, at a given moment, sound. (230)

The chemical metaphor, sustained in part by the word *quintessential* with its alchemical overtones, is never retracted, even as the image of the light in the tunnel is introduced; it only "might have been figured in [Fanny's] mind," and there is no definite commitment to its having happened.

The golden bowl is itself the instrument of Maggie's coming into knowledge of her husband's sexual entanglement with Charlotte Stant, and the breaking of the bowl represents a dramatic culmination of one line of the novel's development. The difference between objects and ideas is that while the bowl can be broken, the knowledge the bowl has introduced into Maggie's mind cannot be dispelled merely by destroying the object. Maggie's consciousness becomes the focalizing tool for volume 2 of the novel, as the Prince's has served to focus much of volume 1, and here James explores Maggie's position in a long passage that again uses metaphor with unusual self-awareness:

> Moving for the first time in her life as in the darkening shadow of a false position, she reflected that she should either not have ceased to be right—that is to be confident—or have recognized that she was wrong; though she tried to deal with herself for a space only as a silken-coated spaniel who has scrambled out of a pond and who rattles the water from his ears. Her shake of the head, again and again, as she went, was much of that order, and she had the resource to which, save for the rude generalizing bark, the spaniel would have been a stranger, of humming to herself hard as a sign that nothing had happened to her. She hadn't, so to speak, fallen in; she had had no accident nor got wet; this at any rate was her pretension until after she began a little to wonder if she mightn't, with or without exposure, have taken cold. (329–30)

The first sentence of the paragraph is bold indeed. "As in the darkening shadow of a false position": the false position is both real and insubstantial, the shadow a mere metaphor but one so ominous it bursts into a simulacrum of something like life. The ante is raised again after the semicolon. The spaniel is already an extravagant metaphor, and the dog is vividly and texturally rendered at the outset ("silken-coated," rattling drops of water, with the shake of the head providing the link between young woman and dog), as well as continuing to lurk throughout the subsequent lines of the passage, if only in negative (Maggie has not fallen in to the water, unlike the notional spaniel). But there is more to come:

> She could at all events remember no time at which she had felt so excited, and certainly none—which was another special point—that so brought with it as well the necessity for concealing excitement. This birth of a new eagerness became a high pastime in her view precisely by reason of the ingenuity required for keeping the thing born out of sight. The ingenuity was thus a private and absorbing exercise, in the light of which, might I so far multiply my metaphors, I should compare her to the frightened but clinging young mother of an unlawful child. The idea that had possession of her would be, by our new analogy, the proof of her misadventure, but likewise all the while only another sign of a relation that was more to her than anything on earth.

It is not surprising that the narrator should perceive a need to offer an apology in advance for the multiplication of metaphors. Maggie is also something like the mother of an illegitimate child, the idea of her husband's infidelity—the tenor of the metaphor—signifying at once the utmost passion ("a relation that was more to her than anything on earth"—as far as the metaphor's vehicle goes, it is the woman rather than the man who has found passion outside marriage) and the utmost shame ("the proof of her misadventure"). It is far-fetched; it draws attention to itself, particularly in the way it so quickly follows on the tail of the spaniel, as it were, and the drama is to that extent conceptual (internal, linguistic) rather than relying on developments in the external world of living breathing characters.

The narrator refers at one point during *The Golden Bowl* to "the final sharp extinction of the inward scene by the outward" (335), and at times we even hear words that turn out not to have been spoken: "some such words as those were what *didn't* ring out," the narrator adds after a passage of dialogue that is in no respect differently marked from the book's other conversational exchanges, "yet it was as if even the unuttered sound had been quenched here in its own quaver" (338). Indeed, James does the exact opposite of the writing-workshop cliché of showing rather than telling: "[Maggie] couldn't have narrated afterwards—and in fact was at a loss to tell herself—by what transition, what rather marked abruptness of change in their personal relation, their drive came to its end with a kind of interval established, almost confessed to, between them" (371). This is quite literally a description of a scene in which *nothing happens*: nothing happens, nothing is confessed, Maggie can't tell herself or anybody else in what this change resides or what exactly prompted or facilitated it, and yet a period has somehow been established in Maggie's relationship with her husband, despite the absence of words for it. This sort of human exchange is exactly what James's fictional language has the wherewithal to notate. Look at this description of Maggie watching the foursome that includes her father, his wife Charlotte and the Prince (Charlotte's lover, Maggie's husband) playing cards, and being struck by

> the fact of her father's wife's lover facing his mistress; the
> fact of her father sitting, all unsounded and unblinking,

between them; the fact of Charlotte keeping it up, keeping up everything across the table, with her husband beside her; the fact of Fanny Assingham, wonderful creature, placed opposite to the three and knowing more about each, probably, when one came to think, than either of them knew of either. Erect above all for her was the sharp-edged fact of the relation of the whole group, individually and collectively, to herself—herself so speciously eliminated for the hour, but presumably more present to the attention of each than the next card to be played. (495)

That is what James's fictional language—his system of notation—is *for*, so to speak: transcribing "the sharp-edged fact of the relation of the whole group, individually and collectively," to each of its members.

One of the many interesting things about James is that he is at once an immensely copious writer and a great novelist of omission. I want to illuminate this paradox of Jamesian style by invoking a contrast drawn by Alan Hollinghurst between Proust's novelistic technique and that of the celebrated—the notorious—stylist Ronald Firbank. In terms of interests and subject matter, Proust and Firbank have a considerable amount in common, Hollinghurst points out, but where Proust is a novelist of almost unprecedented copiousness (I have already suggested that *Clarissa* is the only earlier European novel that can claim to match the scope, richness and intensity of the narrative interiority of *In Search of Lost Time*), Firbank leaves almost everything out:

Where Proust, at just the same time, was expanding the novel to unprecedented length to do justice to his narrator's complex world and his complex consciousness of it, Firbank had arrived at an aesthetic which required almost everything to be omitted. Where Proust, a fellow observer of upper-class society and sexual ambivalence, worked by the endlessly exploratory and comprehensive sentence, the immense paragraph, the ceaselessly dilated book, Firbank laboured to reduce—not merely to condense but to design by elimination. "I am all design— once I get going," he wrote. "I think nothing of filing fifty pages down to make a brief, crisp paragraph, or even a row of dots." He constructed in fragments, juxtaposed without any cushioning or explanatory narrative tissue.[5]

Indeed, the texture of Firbank's fiction is extremely peculiar, skewed by a preference for leaving out what would seem most pertinent. I like this paragraph, from the odd opening chapter of *Concerning the Eccentricities of Cardinal Pirelli*— the failure to identify the object, of which we have learned only that it is not a child despite the fact that we are at a christening, is highly characteristic:

> Beneath the state baldequin, or Grand Xaymaca, his Eminence sat enthroned ogled by the wives of a dozen grandees. The Altamissals, the Villarasas (their grandee-ships' approving glances, indeed, almost eclipsed their wives'), and Catherine, Countess of Constantine, the most talked-of beauty in the realm, looking like some wild limb of Astaroth in a little crushed "toreador" hat round as an athlete's coif with hanging silken balls, while beside her a stout, dumpish dame, of enormous persuasion, was joggling, solicitously, an object that was of the liveliest interest to all.[6]

Proust's manuscript was rejected by any number of publishers, one of whom wrote scathingly that he didn't "see why a man should take thirty pages to describe how he turns over in bed before he goes to sleep."[7] It is not surprising, perhaps: Proust worked in a relatively unorthodox format, writing a book of roughly three thousand pages in an unusual first-person voice that arrogated to itself some of the traits of an omniscient narrator, self-evidently autobiographical and yet also unmistakably fictional rather than factual. The term *roman-fleuve*, used to describe the sort of novel that flows on like a river from one volume to another, is supposed to have been coined by the novelist Romain Rolland, and it is regularly invoked to describe Proust's work as well as other multivolume sequences, such as Anthony Powell's *Dance to the Music of Time*. Writing in the first person, Proust responds to a different set of technical and emotional challenges than James does, but the things he is able to do with the first-person narrator owe a great deal to the nineteenth-century novel's third-person voices, which is one reason I wish to consider him alongside James. Just as much as in James's writing, the characters in Proust are outlined for us as creations of other characters' cognition. As Marcel describes Swann's visits to his great-aunt, consider the movements back and forth between simple description and metaphysical speculation (the translation here is by Lydia Davis, who hews as closely as possible to the contours of Proust's sentences):

No doubt the Swann who was known at the same time to so many clubmen was quite different from the one created by my great-aunt, when in the evening, in the little garden at Combray, after the two hesitant rings of the bell had sounded, she injected and invigorated with all that she knew about the Swann family the dark and uncertain figure who emerged, followed by my grandmother, from a background of shadows, and whom we recognized by his voice. But even with respect to the most insignificant things in life, none of us constitutes a material whole, identical for everyone, which a person has only to go look up as though we were a book of specifications or a last testament; our social personality is a creation of the minds of others. Even the very simple act that we call "seeing a person we know" is in part an intellectual one. We fill the physical appearance of the individual we see with all the notions we have about him, and of the total picture that we form for ourselves, these notions certainly occupy the greater part. In the end they swell his cheeks so perfectly, follow the line of his nose in an adherence so exact, they do so well at nuancing the sonority of his voice as though the latter were only a transparent envelope that each time we see this face and hear this voice, it is these notions that we encounter again, that we hear. (19–20)

Elaborating this conceit, Marcel observes that Swann's "corporeal envelope" has been "so well stuffed" with memories of the time they have all spent together in the country

that this particular Swann had become a complete and living being, and I have the impression of leaving one person to go to another distinct from him, when, in my memory, I pass from the Swann I knew later with accuracy to that first Swann—to that first Swann in whom I rediscover the charming mistakes of my youth and who in fact resembles less the other Swann than he resembles the other people I knew at the time, as though one's life were like a museum in which all the portraits from one period have a family look about them, a single tonality—to that first Swann abounding in leisure, fragrant with the smell of the tall chestnut tree, the baskets of raspberries, and a sprig of tarragon.

One of the things that intrigues me most here is the pacing. Not once but repeatedly the narrator swerves from description to airy speculation, and the generalizations about memory and human cognition are inseparable—or at any rate they couldn't be excerpted without losing a great deal of their power—from the sensory details ("the smell of the tall chestnut tree, the baskets of raspberries, and a sprig of tarragon"). That block of sentences beginning "But even with respect . . ." floats on its own plane, a complex set of lines tethering it to the passage's other levels.

The first section of Proust's immensely long novel describes a coming-into-consciousness, the transformation of the narrator's relationship with the past by way, famously, of the taste of the madeleine. Without that moment, the novelist would never have excavated his own past and allowed it to spring up again to life within himself. "Since what I recalled would have been supplied to me only by my voluntary memory, the memory of the intelligence, and since the information it gives about the past preserves nothing of the past itself," says Marcel, "I would never have had any desire to think about the rest of Combray. It was all really quite dead for me" (44). Recognizing "the taste of the piece of madeleine dipped in lime-blossom tea" that his aunt used to give him, though,

immediately the old gray house on the street, where her bedroom was, came like a stage set to attach itself to the little wing opening onto the garden that had been built for my parents behind it (that truncated section which was all I had seen before then); and with the house the town, from morning to night and in all weathers, the Square, where they sent me before lunch, the streets where I went on errands, the paths we took if the weather was fine. And as in that game enjoyed by the Japanese in which they fill a porcelain bowl with water and steep in it little pieces of paper until then indistinct which, the moment they are immersed, stretch and twist, assume colors and distinctive shapes, become flowers, houses, human figures, firm and recognizable, so now all the flowers in our garden and in M. Swann's park, and the water lilies of the Vivonne, and the good people of the village and their little swellings and the church and all of Combray and its surroundings, all of this which is acquiring form and solidity, emerged, town and gardens alike, from my cup of tea. (47–48)

It is not just form and solidity these scenes acquire; within the image that the narrator introduces here, they are also united by a distinct sensibility insofar as the "firm and recognizable" flowers, houses and figures that appear in the case of the Japanese game are united, not because the objects themselves form part of the same broader category (people are quite different from flowers and buildings) but because they are formed within the same representational sensibility, or in this case with the same technology.[8] It is a sensibility interested in sudden changes of scale; the stage set is scaled almost more like a doll's house, and the bird's-eye view Marcel invokes has the effect of miniaturizing what he describes, reminiscent of the way that tilt-shift photography uses the tactical blurring of selective focus to give, say, a life-sized train in a real-world train station the appearance of being a tiny scale model.

The metaphors in the last section of *The Golden Bowl* continue to be immensely rich and vivid. When Maggie and her father slip off together, "it was wonderfully like their having got together into some boat and paddled off from the shore where husbands and wives, luxuriant complications, made the air too tropical" (511); Maggie tells Fanny Assingham that she wants "a happiness without a hole in it big enough for you to poke in your finger," which inevitably recalls the bowl of the title "as it *was* to have been. . . . The Bowl with all our happiness in it. The bowl without the crack" (483–84). The word that Maggie uses for how she makes things the way she wants them is "humbugging"— an act of imaginative creation, the willful overpowering of reality by thought in a fashion reminiscent of novel-writing, but also, in the context of nineteenth-century American usage, a way of conveying the sense of deliberate deception or manipulation, the tricks of a snake-oil salesman or flim-flam man.

Perhaps the most devastating image in the entire novel is the one used to describe Adam's response to Maggie's revelation, and the nature of the hold he thereby gains on Charlotte; it is mediated through Maggie's consciousness, and it is an extraordinarily vivid and unpleasant simile. In practical terms, the solution that Maggie asks her father to devise involves Charlotte returning to provincial American City with her husband (it is the last place in the world she would have chosen to go, despite the wealth and status that await her there as Adam's wife). Maggie is watching Adam and Charlotte walk about reviewing the items in his collection:

> Charlotte hung behind with emphasized attention; she stopped when her husband stopped, but at the distance of a case or two, or of whatever other succession of objects; and the likeness of their connexion wouldn't have been wrongly figured if he had been thought of as holding in one of his pocketed hands the end of a long silken halter looped round her beautiful neck. He didn't twitch it, yet it was there; he didn't drag her, but she came; and those betrayals that I have described the Princess as finding irresistible in him were two or three mute facial intimations which his wife's presence didn't prevent his

addressing his daughter—nor prevent his daughter, as she passed, it was doubtless to be added, from flushing a little at the receipt of. They amounted perhaps only to a wordless, wordless smile, but the smile was the soft shake of the twisted silken rope, and Maggie's translation of it, held in her breast till she got well away, came out only, as if it might have been overheard, when some door was closed behind her. "Yes, you see—I lead her now by the neck, I lead her to her doom, and she doesn't so much as know what it is, though she has a fear in her heart which, if you had the chances to apply your ear there that I, as a husband, have, you would hear thump and thump and thump. She thinks it *may* be, her doom, the awful place over there—awful for *her*; but she's afraid to ask, don't you see? just as she's afraid of not asking; just as she's afraid of so many other things that she sees multiplied all about her now as perils and portents. She'll know, however—when she does know." (535)

"The smile was the soft shake of the twisted silken rope": no meaningful distinction can be maintained between the metaphor (really present only in language or consciousness) and the smile itself, and once the two have been wrought together, so they will remain. The image is developed even further in the novel's final book:

The thing that never failed now as an item in the picture was that gleam of the silken noose, his wife's immaterial tether, so marked to Maggie's sense during her last month in the country. Mrs. Verver's straight neck had certainly not slipped it; nor had the other end of the long cord—oh quite conveniently long!—disengaged its smaller loop from the hooked thumb that, with his fingers closed upon it, her husband kept out of sight. To have recognized, for all its tenuity, the play of this gathered lasso might inevitably be to wonder with what magic it was twisted, to what tension subjected, but could never be to doubt either of its adequacy to its office or of its perfect durability. These reminded states for the Princess were in fact states of renewed gaping. So many things her father knew that she even yet didn't! (568)

A noose, a tether, a lasso: each term has its own resonance and meanings, layered on top of each other by James (or put in apposition) in an exquisite process that amplifies comprehension rather than producing confusion or blurring the particularities of the situation. It is an interior exteriorizing, a way of tendering those "purely internal states" that Proust, too, deemed the highest and most rewarding subject for the novelist, in a register that is strongly though also always only notionally three-dimensional, dynamic, pictorial: Maggie sees "the picture" as a sort of frozen tableau, even as the tether creates a motivated sense of before and after, of people with a relationship that changes through time.

To return to Proust, Marcel is an advocate for the ethereal over the physical, the representation over the reality, to the extent of wishing to argue that a reader's relationship with characters in books is likely to be richer, fuller, more vivid than any relationship with a living breathing human being encountered in daily life. These are the words developing this line of argument:

When I saw an external object, my awareness that I was seeing it would remain between me and it, lining it with a thin spiritual border that prevented me from ever directly touching its substance; it would volatize in some way before I could make contact with it, just as an incandescent body brought near a wet object never touches its moisture because it is always preceded by a zone of evaporation. In the sort of screen dappled with different states of mind which my consciousness would simultaneously unfold while I read, and which ranged from the aspirations hidden deepest within me to the completely exterior vision of the horizon which I had, at the bottom of the garden, before my eyes, what was first in me, innermost, the constantly moving handle that controlled the rest, was my belief in the philosophical richness and the beauty of the book I was reading, and my desire to appropriate them for myself, whatever that book might be. (85–86)

These afternoons of reading, Marcel continues, "contained more dramatic events than does, often, an entire lifetime":

These were the events taking place in the book I was reading; it is true that the people affected by them were not "real," as Françoise said. But all the feelings we are made to experience by the joy or the misfortune of a real person are produced in us only through the intermediary of an image of that joy or that misfortune; the ingeniousness of the first novelist consisted in understanding that in the apparatus of our emotions, the image being the only essential element, the simplification that would consist in purely and simply abolishing real people would be a decisive improvement. A real human being, however profoundly we sympathize with him, is in large part perceived by our senses, that is to say, remains opaque to us, presents a dead weight which our sensibility cannot lift. (86)

This passage reveals the extent to which Proust was concerned to develop a language for notating interiority. The novelist induces in the reader an intense physiological experience, one in which the novel's characters and incidents occur within us "as we feverishly turn the pages of the book, the rapidity of our breathing and the intensity of our gaze":

> And once the novelist has put us in that state, in which, as in all purely internal states, every emotion is multiplied tenfold, in which his book will disturb us as might a dream but a dream more lucid than those we have while sleeping and whose memory will last longer, then see how he provokes in us within one hour all possible happinesses and all possible unhappinesses just a few of which we would spend years of our lives coming to know and the most intense of which would never be revealed to us because the slowness with which they occur prevents us from perceiving them (thus our heart changes, in life, and it is the worst pain; but we know it only through reading, through our imagination: in reality it changes, as certain natural phenomena occur, slowly enough so that, if we are able to observe successively each of its different states, in return we are spared the actual sensation of change). (87)

Look at the complexity and yet the absolute ease and suppleness of that last sentence: one might think of the parenthetical corollary with which the sentence concludes as bearing some family resemblance to what Flaubert does with the introduction of the aphorism, only in Proust's hands there is no satirical turn; the sentence spirals back over the same ground rather than diverting at a right angle and forging out in a new direction.

The novelist and critic André Aciman (himself an exceptionally gifted stylist) observes that

> the sentence, as conceived—or as *practiced*—by Proust, was not only a vehicle for speaking his melancholy

yearning for things that were, or never were, and might never be again; the sentence was also a medium for decrypting and unpacking, layer after layer, clause after clause, the Russian-doll universe that people turn out to be, Marcel included. The sentence is how Proust sees, or rather how he reveals, that universe. Revelation is key. Description is only interesting insofar as it leads to recognition and surprise.[9]

That, I think, is a very apt way of talking about the effect the previous passage seems to aim for, a sort of sharp poking or prodding of the reader (with no qualms about indulging in repetition or recursivity) into a situation in which insight must be experienced. James is not so much (or not primarily) a novelist of melancholy yearning, but the other observations Aciman makes here might be as persuasively applied to James as to Proust. The other thing about the sentence is that it is a microcosm, or rather we might say—to use a more modern vocabulary—that it partakes of fractal properties, serving as a miniature emblem or replica of the work as a whole. For Austen or Flaubert, the sentence takes on a peculiar force and sharpness that is qualitatively different from what it possesses in the hands of contemporaries such as, say, Sir Walter Scott—for Austen—or Balzac and Émile Zola—for Flaubert. For James and Proust, furthermore, the sentence (or perhaps the paragraph-length block of prose) becomes the unit in which not just the sensibility but also the shape and goals and effects of the whole work of art can most clearly be discerned.

7

Disordered Sentences

Georges Perec, Roland Barthes,
Wayne Koestenbaum, Luc Sante

In my forties, I've become increasingly preoccupied with the ways that books are like the minds of the people who write them. The TV show *Hoarders* has recently drawn widespread attention to what happens when the human instinct to accumulate runs unchecked, and it's clear that the problem doesn't go away when we move from a real world to a virtual one: MP3s, digital books and pictures, movies and emails can also accrete to the point of impeding their owner's ability to get anything done. Only a fine line separates being prolific from experiencing a clinically diagnosable hypergraphia (Alice Flaherty's 2004 book, *The Midnight Disease: The Drive to Write, Writer's Block and the Creative Brain*, offers the best account I know of this disorder); I think often of the famous experiment demonstrating how spiders' webs become

distorted based on which psychotropic drugs they have consumed: amphetamines lead to high-speed web production but
with alarming gaps in the weave; LSD produces beautifully
symmetrical nets with extremely poor functionality. A processing disorder like dyslexia or a compulsive tendency can
contribute to extraordinary acts of creation: the excesses of
Clarissa are intrinsic to the novel's virtues, and I think of
something like Andrew Solomon's books on depression and
childrearing, *The Noonday Demon* and *Far from the Tree*, as
excellent examples of how one type of dyslexia, combined
with a remarkable roving exploratory intelligence, can produce what is almost its own distinctive literary form. Certainly Solomon's writing gives the sense (as in the case studies
of Oliver Sacks) of the most miraculous achievements coming
out of the need to compensate for what would commonly be
considered deficits.

A moment that has stayed with me was when the British historian Boyd Hilton described himself, in a talk that
involved retrospection about the shape of his career, as a
"sad hedgehog and a happy lumper," alluding to the contrast
between his gift for generalization and the narrowness of his
focus on the British evangelical movement in the first half of
the nineteenth century. I had never thought of combining Isa-
iah Berlin's fox–hedgehog paradigm ("The fox knows many
things, but the hedgehog knows one big thing") on a single
pair of axes with Darwin's lumper–hairsplitter opposition,
but it was clear to me at once, as it will be clear to the reader
of this book, that I am a happy fox and a resigned splitter.[1]
As writers, we have to work thoughtfully and realistically
with our weaknesses as well as our strengths. If a humani-
ties dissertation comes in at six hundred pages rather than
two hundred, it doesn't speak to a simple desire to exceed
expectations so much as to something disordered—perhaps
wonderfully disordered, but the logic of accumulation can

become overwhelming (Henry Darger's *Vivian Girls* manuscript is the sort of case I have in mind). At the end of the fourth installment of George R. R. Martin's *Song of Fire and Ice*, the author's afterword reveals that his characters and plot strands have so extremely proliferated that Martin has had to split his draft into two volumes, with the subsequent installment going back to the chronological starting point of this one and following a different set of characters over the same time span ("all the story for half the characters, rather than half the story for all the characters"), and reading this, I saw something of why this particular large-scale project has been so beleaguered with delays and difficulties: when everything tends to grow more complex, or where each plot point is recursively connected to everything else in the work by way of complex patterning, it can become virtually impossible to lay down the entire story in anything like a final form. This is one way of thinking about Samuel Richardson's inability to leave *Clarissa* alone, or about the difficulties James Boswell had deciding what to exclude from the *Life of Johnson*—the sheer mass of paper in the Boswell collections at the Beinecke Library in New Haven provides a vivid demonstration of how hard Boswell found it to let things go.

This language of diagnosis may sound dismissive or even disparaging, but it shouldn't. For certain writers, a condition approaching the clinically diagnosable (a language processing disorder, an obsessive-compulsive streak, a hoarding impulse) can enable the creation of something transcendent, magical, with formal properties both defined and liberated by precisely those constraints. I think of what Roman Jakobson says about metaphor and metonymy in his essay "Two Aspects of Language and Two Types of Aphasic Disturbances": he considers the relationship between contiguity and connection on the one hand and selection or substitution on the other, the former aligned with metonymy and the latter with metaphor, suggesting that almost as clearly as these two poles can be discerned in aphasic language, so they structure literary language, with symbolist poetry standing with metaphor and realist fiction tending to align with the trope of metonymy.[2] In these cases, a new dimension of meaning emerges by way of a formal choice that can be thought of in terms of disorder or constraint. In a canon that includes Austen and James, Flaubert and Proust, the name Georges Perec might have the air of an anomaly. He is much less widely read than those great nineteenth- and early twentieth-century prose writers, and the novel for which he is probably best known in English is famous less for the elegance or craft of its sentences than for eschewing altogether any word that includes the letter *e*. Perec's writings are strongly and idiosyncratically his own, but he is also associated with a Paris-based group called the Ouvroir de Littérature Potentielle (OuLiPo, the Workshop for Potential Literature) whose members were interested in exploring the possibilities of formal constraints in literature, pursuing a playful and yet stringently monastic goal of freedom in constraint.

One thing Perec's work shows with special clarity is the way in which list-making and voluntary constraints, once they take the place of character or plot, may also assume some of the emotional intensity and resonance associated with those components of realist fiction. Here are the opening sentences of Perec's *e*-less novel *La disparition* (1969, translated by Gilbert Adair in 1995 as *A Void*):

Anton Voyl n'arrivait pas à dormir. Il alluma. Son Jaz marquait minuit vingt. Il poussa un profond soupir, s'assit dans son lit, s'appuyant sur son polochon. Il prit un roman, il l'ouvrit, il lut; mais il n'y saisissait qu'un imbroglio confus, il butait à tout instant sur un mot dont il ignorait la signification.

Incurably insomniac, Anton Vowl turns on a light. According to his watch it's only 12.20. With a loud and languorous sigh Vowl sits up, stuffs a pillow at his back, draws his quilt up around his chin, picks up his whodunit and idly scans a paragraph or two; but, judging its plot impossibly difficult to follow in his condition, its vocabulary too whimsically multisyllabic for comfort, throws it away in disgust.[3]

The name the Oulipo writers coined for a text written under a constraint involving the omission of one or more letters was *lipogram*, and perhaps the most distinctive thing about these sentences, on first view, is the oddity of diction brought about by the word choices impelled by the missing vowel. I wrote earlier about "mouthy" sentences, those sequences of words produced by writers like Gary Lutz and Lydia Davis that we roll over on our tongues, but Perec's mode of arresting the reader's attention derives in the first stance from a visual rather than an oral hyperacuity: "mouthy" sentences feel strange when we speak them, but setting up an arbitrary set of constraints to do with letters or representations on the page snags the attention differently, even if the result in both cases is to prevent us from taking the language of the fiction to be fluid or otherwise "natural."

The translation is necessarily quite different from the original; where the French text reads "Son Jaz marquait minuit vingt" (the slangy proper name "Jaz" is necessitated by the fact that the French word for watch is *montre*— *horloge* [clock] is also obviously banned—and the phrase "minuit vingt" feels truncated, abbreviated, absent the word "l'heure"), the English translator can use the more conventional "watch" (because a name brand specific to France, Jaz, wouldn't communicate much to American readers), and he also falls back on transcribing the time in numerals due to the impossibility of writing "twelve twenty" in English without contravening the fundamental rule. Adair has also chosen to narrate in the present tense—the French language has a slightly unusual past tense called the *passé simple*, used only in formal or highly literary writing, that Perec chooses because of the spelling constraint, though it sits oddly with his otherwise highly colloquial style: the *passé composée*, which would be the more colloquial choice, unavoidably relies on the letter *e*.

Both the French and the English sentences remain fully comprehensible—odd but not unrecognizably distorted. Without being warned, one might not at first glance notice the absence of *e*, though I think that the diction alerts the reader to something strange. (Aside from the protagonist's peculiar name, in the French text it is perhaps that sentence about the watch that first flags the reader's attention, while in the English translation, the opening words themselves already invite curiosity—why the curious alliteration, elevated diction and "mouthy" density of "Incurably insomniac"?) Far more extreme is the "complementary" or "reciprocal" text Perec subsequently composed, a novella (it is almost impossible to imagine writing a full-length novel under this constraint) composed of words that use none of the vowels *except e*.[4] This is a much stranger production, ably translated here by Ian Monk (I will in this case give just the English text). The work's French title was *Les Revenentes*, a necessary misspelling (it is the novel of *e*'s retern!), and it was published in English as *The Exeter Text: Jewels, Secrets, Sex* in a collection called *Three By Perec*:

Hélène dwelt chez Estelle, where New Helmstedt Street meets Regents Street, then the Belvedere. The tenement's erne-eyed keeper defended the entrée. Yet, when seven pence'd been well spent, she let me enter, serene.

Hélène greeted me, then served me Schweppes. Cheers!
Refreshments were needed. When she'd devested me, she
herd me eject:

"Phew! The wether!"

"Thirtee-seven degrees!"

"September swelters here."

She lent me her Kleenexes. They stemmed the cheeks'
fervent wetness.

"Well, feel better then?"

Hélène seemed pleesed, yet reserved; expectent re the
recent news. En effet she then begged me:

"Bérengère's entered the See yet?"

"Yes."

"Perfect! Events present themselves well."

These eyes begged her tell me the deserts she expected.
Free jewels?

"Heck, Bérengère's gems 'n' bezels tempt me!" she
yelled.

Her extreme effervescence needed relentment,
meseemed:

"Yet the gems' theft'd be reckless! The See's screened.
Endless tent're there, where expert peelers 'n' shrewd
'tecs dwell. We'd be demented . . ."

"We'll never be checked! We'll detect the defences'
breech, then enter. The rest'll ensew."

Next, she let me redeter her, then tell her the
excerpted speeches the breeze'd sent between the
deserted streets: meseemed rebel men eke lechered
Bérengère's jewels. We regretted the news. Hélène
set her teeth. Her deep verblessness lengthened. The
news'd depressed her? Never, she reneged, then sed
she'd persevere, ne temere. Where led her secret, fervent
reverees? (60–61)

This is style with a vengeance. At moments Perec has created what amounts almost to a new language; although the fluid in question is sweat rather than tears, there is even a certain poignancy to the Kleenex that "stemmed the cheeks' fervent wetness." The fantasy that motivates such literary productions is not a dream of conventional beauty. It is a more cerebral, almost a scientific aesthetic, at times spare but equally capable of playfulness or the sort of baroque bizarrerie seen in the language of *The Exeter Text.*

Perec always displays a keen sense of language as a system of notation or a means of record-keeping—Perec's "day job" involved working as archivist in a scientific laboratory—though there is often, too, a sense of the inevitable failure of language to capture every iota of reality. (Jorge Luis Borges was preoccupied in his stories with the same sorts of representational problem, though those stories differ markedly in feel from Perec's writing.) Here is a paean to miniaturization and precision in "The Page," published in Perec's 1974 collection *Espèces d'espaces* (*Species of Spaces*):

Space begins with that model map in the old editions of the *Petit Larousse Illustré*, which used to represent something like 65 geographical terms in 60 sq. cm., miraculously brought together, deliberately abstract. Here is the desert, with its oasis, its wadi and its salt lake, here are the spring and the stream, the mountain torrent, the canal, the confluence, the river, the estuary, the rivermouth and the delta, here is the sea with its islands, its archipelago, its islets, its reefs, its shoals, its rocks, its offshore bar, and here are the strait, the isthmus and the peninsula, the bight and the narrows, and the gulf and the bay, and the cape and the inlet, and the head, and the promontory, here are the lagoon and the cliff, here are the dunes, here are the beach, and the saltwater lakes, and the marshes, here is the lake, and here are the mountains, the peak, the glacier, the volcano, the spur, the slope, the col, the gorge, here are the plain and the plateau, and the hillside and the hill, here is the town and its anchorage, and its harbour and its lighthouse . . .[5]

The wonderful concreteness of the phrase "something like 65 geographical terms in 60 sq. cm." brings the page vividly to us, with its densely realized geographical features— it is, as Perec goes on to observe, a "pretext for a nomenclature," the list feeling verbal rather than spatial in its conjurations, although the "dictionary space" of the words will be transfigured in the subsequent paragraph into a moving scene ("a long goods train drawn by a steam locomotive passes over a viaduct; barges laden with gravel ply the canals; small sailing boats manoeuvre on the lake"), albeit a scene that still has something of the dollhouse feel of tilt-shift photography.

The epigraph to "The Bed," which follows "The Page" in *Species of Spaces*, offers a distorted version of the famous first line of Proust's novel ("For a long time I went to bed early"): "For a long time I went to bed in writing," attributed to "Parcel Mroust" (16). The piece opens as follows:

We generally utilize the page in the larger of its two dimensions. The same goes for the bed. The bed (or, if you prefer, the page) is a rectangular space, longer than it is wide, in which, or on which, we normally lie longways. "Italian" beds are only to be found in fairy tales (Tom Thumb and his brothers, or the seven daughters of the Ogre, for example) or in altogether abnormal and usually serious circumstances (mass exodus, aftermath of a bombing raid, etc.). Even when we utilize the bed the more usual way round, it's almost always a sign of catastrophe if several people have to sleep in it. The bed is an instrument conceived for the nocturnal repose of one or two persons, but no more.

This is deadpan, playful, ingenious; the mock-pedantic aspect of the commentator's voice is less striking, perhaps, than his unusual clear-eyed insightfulness, which lends poignancy to the discussion. (The effect is almost as destabilizing as Gulliver's disorienting shifts of scale in Lilliput and Brobdingnag.)

The passage is also rendered moving, I think, by the sense of catastrophe being always just round the corner, with that futile "etc." after the two itemized types of catastrophe, one of them a distinctively twentieth-century phenomenon, the other as old as recorded history. Perec was born in 1936 to parents who were Polish Jews but had moved to France in the 1920s. His father died in the French Army in 1940 and his mother died in Auschwitz; Perec himself was sent to live with an aunt and uncle and escaped his mother's end. The fate of the European Jews in the twentieth century shadows much of Perec's work, even when his topic is seemingly unrelated, as in "An Attempt at an Inventory of the Liquid and Solid Foodstuffs Ingurgitated by Me in the Course of the Year Nineteen Hundred and Seventy-Four" (first published in *Action Poétique* in 1976, and reprinted in the collection *L'Infraordinaire*, which was published posthumously in 1989). The text is encompassed in just over five pages of the English-language edition *Species of Spaces and Other Pieces*, and it is my single favorite piece of Perec's. It consists, quite simply, of a list of all of the things eaten by Perec over the course of that calendar year, loosely organized according to the order in which the items might feature on a menu or as components of a conventional meal at a corner bistro or restaurant, arranged within each subcategory in a fashion that is loosely though not restrictively alphabetical: the first entry reads "Nine beef consommés, one iced cucumber soup, one mussel soup" (244), and the list continues through various forms of seafood and vegetable, meat ("One milk-fed lamb, three lamb cutlets, two curried lambs, twelve gigots, one saddle of lamb"), wines, liqueurs and so forth, including a helpless gesture to "N coffees." His biographer, David Bellos, has described Perec as "a man always puzzled by memory and sometimes obsessed with the fear of forgetting," and calls this strange piece an "insane and brilliant inventory-poem" (Perec transcribed the details of what he ate over the course of the year and subsequently organized it into this format): "But even this madly meticulous listing is incomplete," Bellos continues, "for it omits an otherwise unforgettable bottle of 1961 Clos Saint-Denis, drunk with Harry Mathews, out of huge Baccarat glasses."[6] The compulsion to record, Bellos adds, was linked to a sort of breakdown Perec had recently experienced and that drove him to pursue psychoanalysis, a self-described "memory breakdown" which involved the feeling that "unless I made a note of everything, I would be unable to hold on to any part of passing life": "Every evening, with great scrupulousness, with obsessive conscientiousness, I made entries in a kind of log," Perec wrote. "It was an absolutely compulsive procedure! the fear of forgetting!" Lists can perform many functions (canon-formation, self-aggrandizement, celebration), but they also often represent the basic human impulse to hold on to things, to fend off loss by compulsive acts of recording.

The abundance and variety of a Parisian littérateur's eating habits in the 1970s stand in particularly stark contrast to the era of wartime austerity in which Perec spent the earliest parts of his childhood, not to mention to the virtual absence of nourishment that characterized life in the concentration camps. (Is it making too much of an insignificant detail to observe that the very last item on the list reads "three

Vichy waters"?) Perec's own history of loss and displacement is marked, among other places, in his surname itself, as he observes in a short prose proposal called "Ellis Island: Description of a Project" (all these pieces are included in the Penguin *Species of Spaces and Other Pieces*):

I was born in France, I am French, I bear a French first name, Georges, and a French surname, or almost, Perec. The difference is minuscule: there's no acute accent on the first e of my name because Perec is the way the Poles write Peretz. If I had been born in Poland, I would have been called, let's say, Mordecai Perec, and everyone would have known I was a Jew. But I wasn't born in Poland, luckily for me, and I have an almost Breton name which everyone spells as Pérec or Perrec—my name isn't written exactly as it is pronounced.

To this insignificant contradiction there attaches the tenuous but insistent, insidious, unavoidable feeling of being somewhere alien in relation to some part of myself, of being "different," different not so much from "others" as from "my own kin." I don't speak the language that my parents spoke, I don't share any of the memories they may have had. Something that was theirs, which made them who they were, their history, their culture, their creed, their hope, was not handed down to me. (136–37)

The writing-together of the linguistic and the emotional or psychological is characteristic of Perec's approach; he has a keen ear for nuance. But his choices are often those of a writer resistant to emotion. To my eyes, a painful sense of loss hangs over the items in "Attempt at an Inventory," but none of this is *said*, simply created (like certain optical illusions) in the spaces between the page's markings. In some of his longer fictions, Perec adopts a relatively conventional approach of chronological narrative ordering, but he is clearly inclined to disrupt normal procedures wherever possible, so that the fairly straightforward narrative procedure of *A Void* (which is in many respects a kind of detective novel) is enabled or licensed only by the wild tactic of suppressing the *e*. The shorter pieces avoid chronological or conventional forms of ordering almost completely, instead adopting various formal schemes (alphabetic or otherwise) that frequently have a comical topsy-turvy aspect that delights as well as unsettles. In a project inspired by Proust's use of the madeleine at the end of the Combray section of the novel's first volume, Perec admits to having undertaken "to make an inventory, as exhaustive and as accurate as possible, of all the 'Places Where I Have Slept'" and says that he has listed about two hundred:

I haven't yet finally settled on the manner in which I shall classify them. Certainly not in chronological order. Doubtless not in alphabetical order (although it's the only order whose pertinence requires no justification). Maybe according to their geographical arrangement, which would emphasize the 'guidebook' aspect of the work. Or else, according rather to a thematic perspective which might result in a sort of typology of bedrooms:

1. *My* bedrooms
2. Dormitories and barrack-rooms
3. Friends' bedrooms
4. Guest rooms
5. Makeshift beds (settee, moquette plus cushions, carpet, chaise-longue, etc.)
6. Houses in the country
7. Rented villas

8. Hotel rooms
   a. scruffy hotels, boarding houses
   b. luxury hotels
9. Unusual conditions: nights on a train, on a plane, in a car; nights on a boat; nights on guard duty; nights in a police station; nights under canvas; nights in hospital; sleepless nights, etc. (22–23)

Elsewhere, in an appealing and funny piece called "Twelve Sidelong Glances," Perec considers alternatives to the phenomena of fashion. Fashion is seasonal, he observes, but what if it were instead monthly, weekly, daily? "For example," he continues, "there would be Monday clothes, Tuesday clothes, Wednesday clothes, Thursday clothes, Friday clothes, Saturday clothes and Sunday clothes," with the result that "the expression 'today's fashion' would then at last mean exactly what it says" (161).

Perec's works are often puzzling or difficult, but they are also playful, giving them a certain (admittedly perverse) accessibility. *Roland Barthes by Roland Barthes* is a closely contemporary experiment in style, a singularly unorthodox autobiography by the distinguished critic and theorist—also a superlative stylist, and with a playful streak that at times matched Perec's, but working in a mode that foregrounds an aesthetics of difficulty alien to Perec's writing.[7] The broadest literary and intellectual context for this sort of writing might go back to the classic autobiographical narratives of the Western tradition: St. Augustine's *Confessions* and Jean-Jacques Rousseau's, Michel de Montaigne's essays, spiritual autobiographies of the seventeenth and eighteenth centuries, twentieth-century precursors like Jean-Paul Sartre's compelling *The Words (Les Mots)*. It may be worth briefly gesturing to the widespread move that took place in the middle third of the twentieth century away from the representational practices of modernism to a postmodernism increasingly uninterested in the trappings of realism and naturalism. Moving on from Joyce's late writings and the prose and plays of Samuel Beckett, the most prominent body of French literature roughly contemporaneous with Barthes's career might be said to be the *nouveau roman,* whose practitioners (including Sarraute and Robbe-Grillet) wanted to break down everything about the conventional structure of the novel. Barthes's choices in *Roland Barthes by Roland Barthes* may also emerge from a tradition that includes the surrealists' preference for collage; Perec once likened his own practice to William Burroughs's cut-up technique, while Barthes's strange autobiography calls to mind André Breton's troubling and beautiful *Nadja,* with its pastiche of images and words.

Roland Barthes by Roland Barthes is a small book, an engaging oddity. The epigraph reads "It must all be considered as if spoken by a character in a novel" ("Tout ceci doit être considéré comme dit par un personnage de roman," the words reproduced in Barthes's own handwriting), and while the opening sections feature a curious selection of childhood photos, the author announces there will be "only the figurations of the body's prehistory," with pictures ceasing to be reproduced "at the onset of productive life." The project is distinctly Proustian, but where Proust revels and luxuriates in copious sentences, Barthes is a master of ellipsis; he leaves things out, he breaks off unexpectedly, he works by elision and juxtaposition rather than by elaboration. Barthes had experimented elsewhere with unconventional ordering principles (*Le plaisir du texte* is organized alphabetically), and there is a strong alphabetical component to the ordering here as well, with few concessions to chronology or to sustained narrative and small chunks of text organized primarily by keyword instead. The play between indiscretion and discretion provides part of the book's charm, and some of what Barthes reveals remains cryptic, mysterious; there is no guarantee that everything can be decoded.

Some bits, then, to give the feel of the thing. The first is distinctly difficult in terms of the abstraction and subtlety of the thoughts expressed (at times Barthes uses the third person when writing of himself, particularly when discussing his published works):

L'écriture commence par le style ~
Writing begins with style

Sometimes he attempts to use the asyndeton so much admired by Chateaubriand under the name of anacoluthon: what relation can be found between milk and the Jesuits? The following: ". . . those milky phonemes which the remarkable Jesuit, van Ginnekin, posited between writing and language" (*The Pleasure of the Text*). Then there are the countless antitheses (deliberate, farfetched, corseted) and word play from which a whole system is derived (pleasure: *precarious* / bliss: *precocious*). In short, countless traces of the work of *style*, in the oldest sense of the word. Yet this style serves to praise a new value, *writing*, which is excess, overflow of style toward other regions of language and subject, far from a *classed* literary code (exhausted code of a doomed class). This contradiction may perhaps be explained and justified as follows: his way of writing was formed at a moment when the writing of the essay sought a renewal by the combination of political intentions, philosophical notions, and true rhetorical figures (Sartre is full of them). But above all, style is somehow the beginning of writing:

however timidly, by committing itself to great risks of recuperation, it sketches the reign of the signifier. (76)

I can parse some of these sentences, but the paragraph as a whole remains elusive to me. It might be that I resist following Barthes to his conclusion because it finally asserts that even this form of play may be thought of as having an agenda, an ideology of sorts: Barthes's "writing" is a very particular kind of engagement with language and the world, not just a name for the most general form of linguistic play, and though I'm attracted to this idea of "writing" I cannot in the final analysis happily engage in it myself. *Asyndeton* is simply the omission of conjunctions (a classic example can be found in the line *veni, vidi, vici*; "I came, I saw, I conquered"); *anacoluthon* involves a swerve in which a sentence that begins as though it will have one structure changes rules midway, sometimes naming an object that then works as a sort of hinge for the swing or swerve. (It can be either an error or something deliberately sought for its rhetorical effect, the textbook example being drawn from Milton's *Lycidas*—"Had ye been there—for what could that have done?"; Joyce often used it to capture the feel of the stream of a character's consciousness.) The parenthetical aside "(deliberate, farfetched, corseted)" is of course itself an asyndeton, with the surprising nature of the third adjective in the sequence enacting precisely the sort of play that Barthes treats. The distinction between *style* and *writing* is more idiosyncratic, tendentious, harder to follow unless one has steeped oneself in Barthes's work more generally: it has something to do with the luxury or excess of which language is capable.

Passages of abstraction that pose some difficulty to the reader are balanced, both here and elsewhere in Barthes's work, with much more immediately accessible and vivid fragments. The second "bit" I promised appears a page or so after the one I have just quoted (the sequence having progressed alphabetically from *L'écriture* to *L'écrivain*—Howard provides the French subheadings for each of these sections so that the logic of the progression will remain clear to the English-language reader):

L'écrivain comme fantasme ~ The writer as fantasy

Surely there is no longer a single adolescent who has this fantasy: *to be a writer!* Imagine wanting to copy not the works but the practices of any contemporary—his way of strolling through the world, a notebook in his pocket and a phrase in his head (the way I imagined Gide traveling from Russia to the Congo, reading his classics and writing his notebooks in the dining car, waiting for the meals to be served; the way I actually saw him, one day in 1939, in the gloom of the Brasserie Lutétia, eating a pear and reading a book)! For what the fantasy imposes is the writer as we can see him in his private diary, *the writer minus his work:* supreme form of the sacred: the mark and the void. (77–78)

One way of thinking about this difference of manner is to say that Barthes is willing to become novelistic, to extrude particular detail and vivid visual example in order to seduce and pleasure his reader. Elsewhere, he writes:

It is a good thing, he thought, that out of consideration for the reader, there should pass through the essay's discourse, from time to time, a sensual object (as in *Werther*, where suddenly there appear a dish of green peas cooked in butter and a peeled orange separated into sections). A double advantage: sumptuous appearance of a materiality and a distortion, a sudden gap wedged into the intellectual murmur. (135)

The gesture here, in some sense, is simply toward a criticism that engulfs certain properties of the novel. Sensual objects have a place in criticism after all. The green peas in butter, the peeled orange—they make the mouth water, as it were, appealing to the senses rather than purely to the intellect. Barthes enumerates the double effect: "sumptuous appearance of a materiality" (a *sumptuous repast!*), a disruption of the "intellectual murmur."

Elsewhere in the book Barthes characterizes his own style as operating by means of fragments, a choice justified on the grounds that "incoherence is preferable to a distorting order," and attributes his delight in wrestling matches to the fact that each match is itself "a series of fragments, a sum of spectacles . . . subject in its very structure to asyndeton and anacoluthon, figures of interruption and short-circuiting" (93). Along with these figures, Barthes praises parataxis (the placing together of sentences without conjunctions or transitions, in the manner of beads on a string) over hypotaxis (the "subordination" of phrases and sentences, a more shapely or architectural construction). At various points during the book, he contemplates the different sorts of meaning that can be created by way of this kind of technique: the parlor game of taking half-a-dozen words and creating a discourse that links them together (in that case, the fragment in which such a parlor game is defined or described may itself fit the stipulations of the game); the juxtaposition of fragments to create meaning in their interstices, like the lyrics in a song cycle. This sort of "antistructural criticism . . . [brings] objects into view with the help of simple figures of contiguity (metonymies and asyndetons)":

L'ordre dont je ne me souviens plus ~
The order I no longer remember

He more or less remembers the order in which he wrote these fragments; but where did that order come from?

In the course of what classification, of what succession?
He no longer remembers. The alphabetical order erases
everything, banishes every origin. Perhaps in places,
certain fragments seem to follow one another by some
affinity; but the important thing is that these little net-
works not be connected, that they not slide into a single
enormous network which would be the structure of this
book, its meaning. It is in order to halt, to deflect, to
divide this descent of discourse toward a destiny of the
subject, that at certain moments the alphabet calls you
to order (to disorder) and says: *Cut! Resume the story in
another way* (but also, sometimes, for the same reason,
you must break up the alphabet). (148)

"How will I know that the book is finished?" Barthes later
asks.

Having uttered the substance of these fragments for
some months, what happens to me subsequently is
arranged quite spontaneously (without forcing) under
the utterances that have already been made, the structure is gradually woven, and in creating itself, it increasingly magnetizes: thus it constructs for itself, without
any plan on my part, a repertoire which is both finite
and perpetual, like that of language. At a certain
moment, no further transformation is possible but the
one which occurred to the ship *Argo*: I could keep the
book a very long time, by gradually changing each of
its fragments. (162–63)

The word "uttered" has some of the forceful materiality of
the English word "expressed" as it is used to describe the production of breast milk; the process of organization Barthes
describes invokes a series of self-generating patterns, as iron

filings may be shunted into an array by the invisible action of a magnet.[8] Barthes's memoir is contingent rather than inevitable, it could have taken any number of different forms, and yet its distinctive identity (like that of the *Argo*) is established regardless of the contingency of its parts. Here is Barthes at his most Perecian, in a long fragment which I will quote in full:

J'aime, je n'aime pas ~ I like, I don't like

I like: salad, cinnamon, cheese, pimento, marzipan, the smell of new-cut hay (why doesn't someone with a "nose" make such a perfume), roses, peonies, lavender, champagne, loosely held political convictions, Glenn Gould, too-cold beer, flat pillows, toast, Havana cigars, Handel, slow walks, pears, white peaches, cherries, colors, watches, all kinds of writing pens, desserts, unrefined salt, realistic novels, the piano, coffee, Pollock, Twombly, all romantic music, Sartre, Brecht, Verne, Fourier, Eisenstein, trains, Médoc wine, having change, *Bouvard and Pécuchet*, walking in sandals on the lanes of southwest France, the bend of the Adour seen from Doctor L.'s house, the Marx Brothers, the mountains at seven in the morning leaving Salamanca, etc.

I don't like: white Pomeranians, women in slacks, geraniums, strawberries, the harpsichord, Miró, tautologies, animated cartoons, Arthur Rubinstein, villas, the afternoon, Satie, Bartók, Vivaldi, telephoning, children's choruses, Chopin's concertos, Burgundian branles and Renaissance dances, the organ, Marc-Antoine Charpentier, his trumpets and kettledrums, the politico-sexual, scenes, initiatives, fidelity, spontaneity, evenings with people I don't know, etc.

The items on each list are concrete, vivid; they give the sense of a personality. More than that, though, the format of the list—its teasing combination of revelation and withholding—tells us more about Barthes than his expressed dislike for strawberries and women in slacks (Ludwig Wittgenstein also hated it when women wore trousers). A shape or structure is then bestowed on the fragment by the turn in the paragraph that follows:

> *I like, I don't like:* this is of no importance to anyone; this, apparently, has no meaning. And yet all this means: *my body is not the same as yours.* Hence, in this anarchic foam of tastes and distastes, a kind of listless blur, gradually appears the figure of a bodily enigma, requiring complicity or irritation. Here begins the intimidation of the body, which obliges others to endure me *liberally*, to remain silent and polite confronted by pleasures or rejections which they do not share.
>
> (A fly bothers me, I kill it: you kill what bothers you. If I had not killed the fly, it would have been *out of pure liberalism*: I am liberal in order not to be a killer.)

From "anarchic foam" emerges a figure, and yet it is only "the figure of a bodily enigma"—it is the unreadability of the list rather than its cohesion or comprehensibility that interests Barthes, and the parenthetic aside of the final paragraph represents an arabesque of further definition, one that reminds me of Adorno's aphoristic suggestion, in *Minima Moralia*, that "the precondition of tact is convention no longer intact but still present."[9] It is as though Barthes is too courteous to request the reader's empathy, the inconsequential or unreadable aspects of his notation retaining for the writer a discreet corona of privacy.

Perhaps the clearest contemporary descendant of this Barthes, Barthes the sentence-writer, is the American critic and poet Wayne Koestenbaum; at any rate I cannot think of another writer in English who so strongly combines that level of intellectual sharpness with a baroque, sometimes dandyish style and sensibility. Koestenbaum's 1995 book *Jackie Under My Skin: Interpreting an Icon* is difficult to place, generically. It's cultural criticism, for sure, but it's also something like a series of prose poems: the cover of the Plume paperback edition I possess features a familiar photograph of Jackie Kennedy in pink pillbox hat and coat against a luridly acidic green background, the colors drawing the eye and calling to mind the Lilly Pulitzer palette. Each short section has a title—"Jackie and Ordinary Objects," "Jackie and Synesthesia"—and the order of the proceedings is associative, linguistic rather than argument- or narrative-driven in any obvious sense. In musing on how Jackie infuses ordinary objects with meaning, Koestenbaum suggests that press accounts during Jackie's time in the White House emphasized her association with ordinary things partly "because icon Jackie was herself objectified, a commonplace *petite chose* in mass consciousness":

Everything ordinary that Jackie did, owned, or discovered becomes evidence that (1) Jackie is really just one of us, despite her elite veneer; (2) we, despite our relentlessly ordinary lives, are secretly magnificent, because we share plain objects and practices with Jackie; (3) icon Jackie is an unpretentious object in the American home, and that's why she is fond of ordinary things—she identifies with them. Whatnots are her peer group.[10]

It's the last sentence in which Koestenbaum's distinctive style can most clearly be heard—that mouthy "whatnots" catches the attention (a whatnot is much the same thing as a knick-knack, a tchotchke, but it is a far more evocative term in its own right, an arch little word that seems nonetheless to express something fundamental about language, its strengths and its shortcomings). Our relationship with Jackie, Koestenbaum insists, works by contiguity and association: by the trope of metonymy, in which the part stands for the whole and meaning is created by proximity rather than substitution.

Someone quotes Jackie using the word "delish." "Delish"! What an ordinary, slangy word. Jackie said "delish." Maybe Jackie and I have something in common: we share *delish*. We share era-specific conversational banalities. (91)

One hears that Jackie said, while on her restoring mission, "Look at that Lincoln cake plate." What is a cake plate? I didn't know there was a special variety of plate called "cake plate." But Jackie knew, and she pointed to it. "Cake plate" becomes another molecule in the Jackie pointillism—another detail, mysterious, unsymbolic, that helps to compose icon Jackie. (93)

"Jackie and Synesthesia" offers a fuller vision of what this sort of cultural criticism might do. Synesthesia simply refers to the neurological phenomenon by which an object conventionally comprehensible in one sense is perceived in terms of another (letters or numbers and colors, smells or tastes and sounds—recent research suggests that mild forms of synesthesia are much more prevalent than previously believed). *Synesthesia* the term thus becomes the license for unbridled association—synesthesia "permits us to reconstruct Jackie," Koestenbaum says, and then he moves into an extraordinarily baroque associative fugue: "For example, when I think 'Jackie,' or see a picture of Jackie, several objects, confections, or incidental 'treasures' (as Jackie might have called them) come to mind. I think of the perfume called Jicky, by Guerlain; I think of Chiclets chewing gum; I think of petits fours; and I think of enameled clip-on earrings" (195). In subsequent paragraphs, Koestenbaum delves deeply into each of these terms ("The name 'Jicky' itself seems halfway between 'Jackie' and 'sticky.' The idea that a product called Jicky exists, waiting to be bought, excites me: icon Jackie behaves like a product but one can't buy her, she is off the market"). The sound of the words themselves is as crucial here as the senses they serve:

> Petits fours: petits fours are the sort of French dessert (like mille-feuille) that in the 1960s I considered fancy. Petits fours are square, with hard butter-cream frosting and soft tea cake inside, lined with jam. The inside of a petit four isn't a treat; its outside is—for the same reason (hardness, resistance, sheen) that the coat of a Chiclet pleases. I have always liked sugary glazes, and therefore appreciate petits fours, or the idea of petits fours, via the word "glacé," which enters the sphere of Jackie through the kid gloves she wore to the Inaugural Ball, described in one account as "20 button white glacé kid gloves" which successfully avoided "wrinkle or downward sag." The gloves' perfection—no wrinkle, no sag—comes by virtue of the property called "glacé." A second route through which "glacé" and "Jackie" meet, in my imagination, is through the word "chignon." I think of Jackie's classic bouffant as a chignon: the word "chignon" (whose origin is "chain") recalls a kind of glazed cruller shaped like a twist (were they called "glazed twists" or "French twists"?). (196–97)

This is brilliantly associative, and also willfully unmotivated by anything other than the feel of words in the mouth (it is surely not coincidental that so many of these words are also *for* things that one savors on the tongue, or perhaps I too am excessively partial to sugary glazes?).

The *Jackie* book does seem to form a network of meaning; elsewhere, Koestenbaum takes even further Barthes's injunction to cut things up, to work in fragments. In "My '80s," he serves up an autobiography in fragments; it is an essay I mentally juxtapose to an equally striking though quite different short prose piece by Luc Sante, "Commerce," which also chronicles a time and a place—New York at the end of the 1970s—long gone.[11] Neither "My '80s" nor "Commerce" is an exercise in nostalgia (as Carl Wilson says, "Nostalgia tends to neuter critique").[12] Both pieces adopt a nonchronological method of ordering: Koestenbaum's sentences are more show-offy, extravagant, while Sante works in an understated idiom that at times seems even to forego style altogether (in the sense that the accoutrements of classic noir proclaim themselves less style than antistyle). Koestenbaum sometimes adopts Oulipian methods (he is partial to the sort of "I remember" refrain pioneered by Joe Brainard in 1970 and played with by Perec and Kenneth Koch, among others, before Harry Mathews adopted it for his "remembrance" of Georges Perec in *The Orchard*, published in French in 1986 and in English translation in 1988), but here he is surely writing under the sign of Barthes and of Susan Sontag, whose expressed preference (in "Notes on 'Camp'") for "the form of jottings, rather than an essay" as she tries to capture "this particular fugitive sensibility" (276–77) provides another kind of license for Koestenbaum's modus operandi ("I swore allegiance to the aphorism," Koestenbaum writes at one point [133]). Here are a few of his fragments:

My mind was on *écriture feminine* as applied to homosexuals. I was big on the word "homosexual." I read *Homosexualities and French Literature* (edited by George Stambolian and Elaine Marks). I read Hélène Cixous. On a train I read *Roland Barthes by Roland Barthes* (translated by Richard Howard): I looked out dirty windows onto dirty New Jersey fields. I began to take autobiography seriously as a historical practice with intellectual integrity. On an airplane I read Michel Leiris's *Manhood* (translated by Richard Howard) and grooved to Leiris's mention of a "bitten buttock"; I decided to become, like Leiris, a self-ethnographer. I read Gide's *The Immoralist* (translated by Richard Howard) in Hollywood, Florida, while lying on a pool deck. I read many books translated by Richard Howard. In the '80s I read *The Fantastic* by Tzvetan Todorov (translated by Richard Howard) and meditated on the relation between fantasy and autobiography. I brought Richard Howard flowers the first time I met him (1985), in his book-lined apartment. He assured me that I was a poet. (128–29)

Too many of these sentences begin with the first-person singular pronoun. Later I may jazz up the syntax, falsify it. (129)

Despite my best efforts, I existed in history, not as agent but as frightened, introspective observer. I began to fine-tune my sentences—a fastidiousness I learned from Moore's prose. Precise sentences were my ideals, though in practice I was slipshod and sentimental. I began to seek a balance between improvisation and revision. I revised by endlessly retyping. (133)

The balance between mind, eye and ear here is striking and unusual. In the first fragment, for instance, the cerebral flourish of the initial sentence is self-mockingly deflated by its more "mouthy" successor (the meaning comes through because of the feel of the words in the mouth, helped out by those slightly campy quotation marks). The repetition of Richard Howard's name is humorous and affectionate while the mention of a specific year in parenthesis is undermined by its location immediately following a rumination on the relationship between autobiography and fantasy. The fragment refuses cadence, structure as a whole—it is a paratactic collection of sentences, a sequence rather than a structure. But these longer paratactic fragments are also balanced by shorter, sharper ones, more aphoristic reflections, reflections with a shape: this is the explicit subject, indeed, of the second fragment given earlier, in which syntax is *jazzed up* and *falsified*, the kind of cutting or syncopation that Barthes commends. The sentence "I revised by endlessly retyping" is not perhaps an aphorism as such, but it has the cadence of aphorism; it summarizes and punctuates the fragment it curtails. The cumulative effect of the piece as a whole is something I cannot do justice to here, but it produces a curiously moderated form of self-knowledge, a few parts pathos tincturing the near-clinical self-examination: auto-ethnography conducted under the sign of style.

"My '80s" could never be mistaken for a short story; its allegiance is more clearly to the essay, despite its unorthodox shape and structure. (It is possible that I am predisposed to think this because of its subsequent inclusion in the *Best American Essays* volume, but the piece was originally published in *Artforum*, and these two sites of publication confirm the reader's sense that this is autobiographical criticism, and in that sense nonfiction.) Sante's "Commerce," on the other hand, feels much more like a short fiction, though I have the impression, as a reader, that everything he writes there is true to the best of his knowledge. The title conjures up notions of buying and selling and exchange but also that eighteenth-century sense of commerce as something close to conversation: this ethnography will not center on the author himself but on transactions he observed. The whole piece feels more clearly selected, crafted, shaped than Koestenbaum's (Koestenbaum is an artist of excess, Sante one of concision), so that taking pieces out of it does more comparative violence in this case to the shape and meanings of the piece as a whole, but here are a few of my favorite fragments:

One morning as I was walking up First Avenue, a dog ran past me with a dollar bill in its mouth. A few seconds later a fat man came puffing by in hot pursuit. (102)

For years there was a general store, of the most traditional sort, on 9th and Second. I did my photocopying there, bought aspirin, string, drywall screws, mayonnaise, and greeting cards on various occasions. You could not imagine that they could possibly carry the exact spice or piece of hardware or style of envelope you needed, since the place was not enormous, but invariably an employee would disappear into some warren and re-emerge with your item in hand. In my memory I am always going there during blizzards. Another sort of general store stood on the corner of 14th and Third. It may have had another name, but its sign read "Optimo." It was cool and dark inside, with racks of pipes and porn novels and shelves of cigar boxes and candy. Of its two display windows on 14th Street, one featured scales, glassine envelopes, and bricks of Mannitol—the Italian baby laxative favored by dealers in powder for stretching their merchandise—and the other held shields, badges, and handcuffs. I often wished that Bertolt Brecht had been alive to admire those windows. (106–7)

Meaning here is created not by the selection of words in the sentence but by the juxtaposition of sentences and the choice—the paratactic choice—to sequence these bits like beads on a string, rather than subordinating them into an essay with a clear beginning, middle and end. The chaos and senselessness of this New York emerge, and yet also the patterns that create meaning out of disorder. I would say that there is no argument here, not even an oblique one. Neither is there a story. It is an exercise in seeing what's left when we take away all the conventions and continuities of storytelling, leaving only the bare identities of time and place as the framework for stimulating intellectual and emotional response.

The final fragment is deliberately incomplete and yet horribly conclusive:

When S. inherited his father's estate, although it was not a major sum, he promptly retired. That is, he quit his job, moved into a room in the George Washington Hotel on 23rd Street, and took his meals at the doughnut shop on the corner. He read, wrote, strolled, napped. It was the life of Riley. He might have continued in this fashion indefinitely had he not made the acquaintance of cocaine. (112)

This is a highly ascetic choice for closure—Sante resists even the temptation to use the foreboding dot-dot-dot of an ellipsis in this conclusion in which nothing is concluded. We are left in a curious tense, an ongoing past which we know must have found its period not long afterward, a tense that refuses pathos and melodrama and leaves us instead with the structural sense that this piece is a kind of ourobouros, its tail clamped delicately between its teeth. The emotional drama emerges entirely from the tension between the author's desire to record and retain these ephemera—"these fragments have I shored against my ruin"—and the spare verbal aesthetic, in which no superfluous word is allowed to remain in the prose. As different as "Commerce" is from Perec's "Attempt at an Inventory," both memorialize in list-like format as a way of locating and describing an intense sense of loss. These short prose forms fall between essay and story, and for me they capture something especially pressing and poignant about human life, its compulsions and tics; they also underline the extent to which even the deepest consolations of reading and writing can only ever be partial or inadequate.

8

Details That Linger and the Charm of Voluntary Reading

George Pelecanos, Stephen King, Thomas Pynchon

A lighter interlude after that solemn conclusion: not all is lost. Certain details linger in the mind long after the novels in which they appear have largely faded from memory. Here, for instance, is a sentence that I can't quite decide whether I love or hate. It is a line from Julia Glass's *Three Junes*, a man's description of fixing a puppy's hernia by hand when he was a boy: "I still recall the sensation of pushing the lump of flesh back through the muscle wall in that taut little belly, using just the tip of my right middle finger. It felt like forcing a marble into an elastic velvet pouch."[1] I am tempted to adduce it as a happy instance of self-consciously "fine" writing mobilized in the service of character development and the themes of the novel as a whole, and yet there is something gratuitous, distracting, self-indulgent about it. It seems to me costly to stud one's narrative prose with observations of this sort, though it's probably easier to get away with it in a first-person narrative than when writing in the third person; in the latter case, the author risks losing the goodwill of a reader who may prefer not to be asked to admire the author's own lavish powers of noticing and notating.

Another kind of memorable novelistic detail figures in the world of history or human psychology rather than existing primarily in the register of style or as a turn of phrase. I have two favorite examples of this sort of detail, instances I think of very regularly; I suppose one might accumulate a much larger collection, but these two are memorable particularly for being at once minor, even insignificant and at the same time sweepingly effective in terms of establishing some aspect of a setting or a relationship. In George Pelecanos's novel *Hard Revolution*, set in Washington, D.C., in the late 1960s, the protagonist walks into a diner called the Three-Star: "Ella Lockheart, the Three-Star's counter-and-booth waitress, poured watery A&P brand ketchup into bottles marked Heinz."[2] It's an unassuming detail; this is a very ordinary part of the quotidian routine in a familiar location, something you might well see happening if you stop by a diner regularly. But it very nicely conjures something of the down-market nature, the casual acceptance of deception, the inherent seediness of the physical and moral milieu in which the story is set. The specificity of the detail is verbal as well as visual: A&P is a name evocative for me not just of the John Updike story of that title but of the years I spent as a young child in 1970s Wilmington, Delaware, where people said "I'm going to the A&P" as though it were synonymous with "going to the grocery store."

My other example is drawn from Stephen King's *Needful Things*, a novel whose plot involves a sinister antique store where purchasers can buy whatever it is they most need, but

only at the cost of their souls. What the novel's female protagonist craves is relief from the pain of severe arthritis in her
hands. Her boyfriend is the town cop: he is an observant and
perceptive man who knows that dialing a telephone is physically very painful for her, even on a good day but especially on
a bad day. When he sees her dial a number and doesn't hear
pain in her voice, he accordingly makes the wrong judgment
about what sort of day she is having: "because she was on the
far side of the room," the unobtrusive third-person narration
coolly runs, "he was unable to see that this phone—and all the
others—had been changed earlier that day to the type with the
oversized fingerpads."[3] Taken out of context, this is a neutral
detail, but in the context of the story, it is intensely ominous,
the first of a number of ordinary small misjudgments and
mishaps that rapidly escalate into the kind of supernatural
catastrophe whose depiction is one of King's specialties. This
detail would translate effectively into a language other than
English, although I suppose the passage of time may have rendered landline telephones, with or without oversized keypads,
relatively little known to a younger generation; it is much less
grounded in specifics of time and place, at any rate, than the
ketchup example of the previous paragraph.

Tim Parks has recently argued that in the contemporary
world of literature, pressures both internal and external tend
to push writers in the direction of less complexity, with many
novelists "perform[ing] a translation within their own languages" or "discover[ing] a lingua franca within their own
vernacular, a particular straightforwardness, an agreed order
for saying things and perceiving and reporting experience,"
with the consequence of making translation of a novel from
one language to another "easier and more effective," but only
at a high cost in terms of the linguistic originality and complexity of the prose.[4] He regrets the move away from forms of
writing he sees as having been more resistant to this sort of

easy seamless transition, writing that embraced idiosyncratic vernaculars without regard to the consequences for international markets. "Above all there is a problem with a kind of writing that is, as it were, inward turning, about the language itself," he writes, "about what it means to live under the spell of this or that vernacular":

> Of course one can translate Joyce's *Ulysses*, but one loses the book's reveling in its own linguistic medium, its tireless exploration of the possibilities of English. The same is true of a lot of the experimental writing of the 1960s and 1970s. It is desperately hard to translate the Flemish writer Hugo Claus into English, or indeed *Gravity's Rainbow* into anything. There was a mining of linguistic richness in that period, and a focus on the extent to which our culture is made up of words, that tended to exclude, or simply wasn't concerned about, the question of having the text travel the world. Even practitioners of "traditional" realism like John Updike or, in England and in a quite different way, Barbara Pym, were obsessively attentive to the exact form of words that was their culture.

Parks sees the move away from exactitude toward lingua franca as having been especially costly for writers working initially in languages other than English, but it may be that English-language writers too have "skeletonized" their own idioms, eradicating the sorts of specificity that would prevent their novels from slipping easily into other languages via the medium of translation. In a 2005 interview with Tim Adams for the *Observer*, Kazuo Ishiguro claimed a sort of globalized impulse for himself, one that he said affected his choices as a stylist: "I want my words to survive translation. I know when I write a book now I will have to go and spend three days being intensely interrogated by journalists in Denmark or wherever. That fact, I believe, informs the way I write—with those Danish journalists leaning over my shoulder."[5]

Ishiguro's fiction does seem unusually open to being translated; his sentences are very beautifully constructed, but they are largely stripped of the sort of linguistic particularity that would provoke difficulties for the translator. To return to Tim Parks's counterexample, *Gravity's Rainbow* provides a very good instance of verbal particularity posing unusual challenges to the potential translator, not least because of its intense American-ness, the affectation of a jaunty and demented 1940s idiom that owes much to the sound of movies and popular music. Here is a bit of Pynchon's prose, a favorite of mine, that shows very clearly the sort of "reveling in [a] linguistic medium" that Parks has in mind. Brigadier Ernest Pudding is "rambling on from the pulpit" of what was once a private chapel in the house that gives shelter to the divisions of "The White Visitation":

> The mud of Flanders gathered into the curd-clumped, mildly jellied textures of human shit, piled, duckboarded, trenched and shell-pocked leagues of shit in all directions, nor even the poor blackened stump of a tree—and the old blithering gab-artist tries to shake the cherry-wood pulpit here, as if that had been the worst part of the whole Passchendaele horror, that absence of vertical interest. . . . On he goes, gabbing, gabbing, recipes for preparing beets in a hundred tasty ways, or such cucurbitaceous improbabilities as Ernest Pudding's Gourd Surprise—yes, there *is* something sadistic about recipes with "Surprise" in the title, chap who's hungry wants to just *eat* you know, not be Surprised really, just wants to bite into the (sigh) the old potato, and be reasonably sure there's nothing inside *but* potato you see, certainly not

some clever nutmeg "Surprise!", some mashed pulp all
magenta with *pomegranates* or something . . .[6]

The ellipsis is in the original passage, as are the italics; it goes
on for many more sentences in this vein. That first sentence is
quite "mouthy," in a Lutzian way (it is characteristic of this
novel, with its anal obsessions and its scenes of coprophagy,
that mouthiness should arrive in a sequence of words like "the
curd-clumped, mildly jellied textures of human shit"). The
exact words matter here: "piled, duckboarded, trenched and
shell-pocked" register as strongly as a syllabic sequence as
they do in terms of establishing a physical environment, and
the same can be said as the tone shifts away from Pudding's
own words to the exterior voice of some unnamed audience
member whose consciousness filters the next bit of the passage. The phrase "cucurbitaceous improbabilities," punctu-
ating a sustained study in voice that relies on the rhythms
of colloquial speech: what could be more gratuitous? It isn't
functional, it's not load-bearing: it is a form of narrative play
that would pose enormous difficulties if one were to wish to
capture the same effects in another language. In its encyclope-
dic wordplay, Pynchon's great novel harks back to *Moby-Dick*
and *Ulysses* both; for me, it doesn't quite match the sublimity
of Melville's novel (or indeed of *Paradise Lost*, another major
epic it sometimes calls to mind), but it exceeds *Ulysses* on certain counts, not least in the propulsive purposefulness of the
story. Daniel Mendelsohn has recently put into words something of what I dislike about *Ulysses* (his observations were
included at *Slate* as part of a larger collection of critics' and
writers' thoughts on what "great books" may be overrated):

Honestly I've never been persuaded by *Ulysses*. To my
mind, Joyce's best and most genuine work is the wonderful *Dubliners*; everything afterwards smacks of striving

to write a "great" work, rather than simply striving to write—it's all too *voulu*. Although there are, of course, beautiful and breathtakingly authentic things in the novel (who could not love that tang of urine in the breakfast kidneys?), what spoils *Ulysses* for me, each time, is the oppressive allusiveness, the wearyingly overdetermined referentiality, the heavy constructedness of it all.[7]

He compares the experience of reading *Ulysses* to "being on one of those Easter egg hunts you went on as a child— you constantly feel yourself being *managed*, being carefully steered in the direction of effortfully planted treats." It is undoubtedly the case that my love for *Gravity's Rainbow* and my dislike for *Ulysses* derive partly from the stages of life at which I encountered them: it was probably only two or three years apart, but *Gravity's Rainbow* was something I found on my own in the treasure trove of the library, and reading it felt transgressive and exciting because of its subject matter and how very different it was from the novels one read in high school English classes (*Jane Eyre*, *The Great Gatsby*), while *Ulysses* has had the misfortune to become entrenched as part of an undergraduate curriculum that has more of the flavor of responsibility to a tradition than of free-ranging play. I envy my students who love *Ulysses* because it seems to them to have some transgressive promise, but that is not the book I have been required to read, and I side with Daniel Mendelsohn in finding the freshness and force of *Dubliners* immensely more precious.

9

The Ideal Bookshelf

The Rings of Saturn and
The Line of Beauty

In October 2012, Hurricane Sandy hit New York. In Morningside Heights, I found myself virtually unaffected, but A. and her twelve-year-old son O. (plus cat José Reyes) had to evacuate their West Street apartment and stay in my living room for a week. A. and I have been best friends since our first week at university, in 1988, and I can honestly say that our only major point of disagreement in life concerns the Oxford comma (she is pro, I am vehemently con). That week immediately preceded the presidential election, making A.'s job as a senior editor at the *New Yorker* particularly demanding. The New York City public schools were closed all week, and O. and I went for runs and inspected hurricane damage in Riverside Park, ate bagels, watched *Firefly*, the first season of *Fringe* and *The Big Bang Theory* and baked a cake—a lifestyle sufficiently suited to our mutual tastes that O. observed, at the end of the week, that he thought he might want to be a professor when he grew up. As a thank-you present, A. and O. commissioned a painting for me, an "Ideal Bookshelf": artist Jane Mount paints portraits of people through the spines of their favorite books, in gouache and ink on smooth water-color paper. Mine includes many of the books I write about in these pages—Richardson's *Clarissa* and Austen's *Pride and Prejudice*, Burke's *Reflections* and Goffman's *Presentation of Self in Everyday Life*, Burgess's *99 Novels* and Rebecca West's extraordinary *The Fountain Overflows* (perhaps my favorite novel of all time, paired with James Baldwin's *Just Above My Head* in the innermost recess of my heart)—but also several more personal choices: *Fire and Hemlock*, by Diana Wynne Jones, which seems to me to capture the emotional tone of growing up better than any book I know, and Dick Francis's novel *The Danger*. It is not his best novel, but it is one I possess in a signed hardcover first edition because my idolatry of Dick Francis at age twelve was such that my mother let me take half a day off school to attend his book signing in Center City.

I am sufficiently a novel-reader at heart that though Perec is one of my favorite writers, he never wrote a book that could be described as one of my favorite novels; in fact, I have to confess, shamefully, that I have never read *Life: A User's Manual* in its entirety. There are a small handful of books, though, that seem to me to provide the fullest possible range of pleasures: the mandarin satisfactions of sentence-writing, the emotional and affective richness of fiction in the tradition of Eliot or Dickens, the aching sense of dislocation or loss that might be associated more with William Wordsworth or Paul Celan than with fiction as such. The two I'll write about here both feature on my ideal bookshelf: the German writer W. G. Sebald's *The Rings of Saturn* and the English novelist and critic Alan Hollinghurst's *The Line of Beauty*. They seem to me to represent the culmination of what can be done in each of two major lines of style that emerge from the nineteenth-century European literary tradition: the inward turn of the Proustian first-person voice in Sebald's case; in Hollinghurst's, the elaborations and acts of judgment associated with the use of the third-person voice by George Eliot and Henry James.[1] Sebald's book (it is not exactly a novel, rather a web- or netlike construction of equivocally fictional species, owing something to Thomas Bernhard's crypto-autobiographical first-person voices and even more to the reflexive fictions of Jorge Luis Borges) can be thought of as testing the limits of what might be done with a first-person voice in the Proustian tradition, although the relationship with memory is here quite different. The impersonal first-person voice has been largely emptied out of all distinguishing traits, and serves primarily as a kind of repository for collective memory, calling Perec more strongly to mind than Proust. Hollinghurst's novel is explicitly and outrageously Jamesian, a technically extraordinary accomplishment that is at once highly conservative and radically fresh in its language and subject matter; the novel's third-person narration prominently features the sorts of satirical summing-up voices, the ability to swoop in and out of the thoughts of a focalizing character, that might seem to have disappeared from the novel as the nineteenth century turned into the twentieth, a form of narration that Hollinghurst shows to be an exceptionally powerful aesthetic and moral instrument. Both books, though, as different as they may seem on the face of things, share Jamesian *and* Proustian elements, showing clearly the cross-pollination of these two lines of style, each offering a unique set of advantages for chronicling loss and delineating the devastation wrought by an epidemic or a conscious program of eradication.

When talking about Sebald, it's tempting to use the term *sensibility* rather than style as such, especially as I am not capable of reading his books in the original German; on the other hand, Sebald very closely supervised their translations, having taught literature at an English university for most of his career. Sebald was born in 1944 and grew up in a postwar Germany of silences and forgetting. He writes between fact and fiction (I think, too, of Naipaul's *The Enigma of Arrival*), and the photographs with which his texts are interspersed, as in Barthes's curious autobiography, represent not so much a means of corroboration (*I was there*) as a device for calling into question what we think we know. They are curious, sideways, elliptical; they institute the slippage and blurring of fact rather than its fixity, with details often askew. Sebald's texts have the patina of verisimilitude but cannot in any straightforward sense be thought of as nonfiction. Unlike other equally "literary" or well-crafted pieces of prose that are more clearly nonfictional—I am thinking here in particular of Primo Levi's masterpiece *The Periodic Table*—the narratorial persona is definitively though non-pin-down-ably different from the real-world historical figure of the author himself, despite what the two may have in common (the divergence feels wider, I think, than in the case of Bernhard).

Sebald published a nonfiction book called *On the Natural History of Destruction*, about writing and memory in the wake of the Allied bombing of Dresden during World War II, and that title phrase offers one avenue of entry into the strange and fascinating book that is *The Rings of Saturn*. Though *The Rings of Saturn* describes the narrator's walking tour around East Anglia, it also concerns the death of Jews in the European camps (Sebald's family had Jewish connections, though his father fought in the German army and spent the last part of the war in a prisoner of war camp), the European war in the air, citywide firestorms. One of the characters the narrator meets and converses with is a gardener named William Hazel who remains obsessed, some sixty years later, with the bombing raids launched on Germany from "the sixty-seven airfields that were established in East Anglia after 1940":

Pepple nowadays hardly have any idea of the scale of the operation, said Hazel. In the course of one thousand and nine days, the eighth airfleet alone used a billion gallons of fuel, dropped seven hundred and thirty-two thousand tons of bombs, and lost almost nine thousand aircraft and fifty thousand men. Every evening I watched the bomber squadrons heading out over Somerleyton, and night after night, before I went to sleep, I pictured in my mind's eye the German cities going up in flames, the firestorms setting the heavens alight, and the survivors rooting about in the ruins. One day when Lord Somerleyton was helping me prune the vines in this greenhouse, for something to do, said Hazel, he explained the Allied carpet-bombing strategy to me, and some time later he brought me a big relief map of Germany. All the place names I had heard on the news were marked in strange letters alongside symbolic pictures of the towns that varied in the number of gables, turrets and towers according to the size of the population; and moreover, in the case of particularly important cities, there were emblems of features associated with them, such as Cologne cathedral, the Römer in Frankfurst, or the statue of Roland in Bremen. Those tiny images of towns, about the size of postage stamps, looked like romantic castles, and I pictured the German Reich as a medieval and vastly enigmatic land. Time and again I studied the various regions on the map, from the Polish border to the Rhine, from the green plains of the north to the dark brown Alps, partly covered with eternal snow and ice, and spelled out the names of the cities, the destruction of which had just been announced: Braunschweig and Würzburg, Wilhemlshaven, Schweinfurt, Stuttgart, Prorzheim, Düren, and dozens more. In that way I got to know the whole country by heart; you might even say it was burnt into me. (38–39)

This excerpt shows how important the technique of collage is for Sebald—he incorporates others' words, together with photographs and often topographical descriptions, into a sort of pastiche. The preoccupation with questions of scale is also highly characteristic of Sebald's approach, here and elsewhere, as is the loving description of the large relief map in which one can see all of Germany in miniature, with those strange emblems the size of postage stamps.

Sebald frequently gestures to seventeenth- and eighteenth-century styles—most notably to Sir Thomas Browne's *Religio Medici*, though with meanderings also reminiscent of Burton's *Anatomy of Melancholy* and Montaigne's *Essays*—but the book is patently less early modern than postmodern in its instabilities and uncertainties. The rambling walking tour the narrator embarks upon at the book's outset is without a clear purpose other than to dispel the "emptiness" that takes hold of him after the completion of a long stint of work. (3). The book itself is composed under the shadow of the deaths of several university colleagues, including a lecturer in Romance languages named Janine Dakyns:

Janine had taken an intense personal interest in the scruples which dogged Flaubert's writing, that fear of the false which, she said, sometimes kept him confined to his couch for weeks or months on end in the dread that he would never be able to write another word without compromising himself in the most grievous of ways. Moreover, Janine said, he was convinced that everything he had written hitherto consisted solely in a string of the most abysmal errors and lies, the consequences of which were immeasurable. Janine maintained that the source of Flaubert's scruples was to be found in the relentless spread of stupidity which he had observed everywhere, and which he believed had already invaded his own head. It was (so supposedly he once said) as if one was sinking into sand. (7)

The narrator moves through an associative summary of Janine's thoughts on sand in Flaubert into a vivid description of the setting for his and Janine's regular conversations about Flaubert, an office so flooded with paper that "a virtual paper landscape had come into being in the course of time, with mountains and valleys" (8). This "amazing profusion of paper" is another replica, a scale model of some geological catastrophe, a thing of beauty as well as of terror: in this case the narrator moves on through an image of Janine amidst her papers resembling "the angel in Dürer's *Melancholia*, steadfast among the instruments of destruction" to Janine referring him to a surgeon who might know something about the whereabouts of the skull of Sir Thomas Browne. The prose runs continuously, with few paragraph breaks and punctuated only by the occasional photographic reproduction, touching down at one unexpected place after another and arriving at a description of Rembrandt's painting *The Anatomy Lesson*, a picture that casts doubt (so the narrator argues, at any rate—I have hotly disputed the question of the orientation of the hand with my own students!) on its own verisimilitude:

Contrary to normal practice, the anatomist shown here has not begun his dissection by opening the abdomen and removing the intestines, which are most prone to putrefaction, but has started (and this too may imply a punitive dimension to the act) by dissecting the offending hand. Now, this hand is most peculiar. It is not only grotesquely out of proportion compared with the hand closer to us, but it is also anatomically the wrong way round: the exposed tendons, which ought to be those of the left palm, given the position of the thumb, are in fact those of the back of the right hand. In other words, what we are faced with is a transposition taken from the anatomical atlas, evidently without further reflection, that turns this otherwise true-to-life painting (if one may so express it) into a crass misrepresentation at the exact centre point of its meaning, where the incisions are made. (16–17)

This sense of deep unreliability or instability in vision is all-pervasive in *The Rings of Saturn*. The narrator is obsessed with technologies of viewing, their powers and their limits, as when he sits down on a bench and looks out to sea:

I felt as if I were in a deserted theatre, and I should not have been surprised if a curtain had suddenly risen before me and on the proscenium I had beheld, say, the 28th of May 1672 that memorable day when the Dutch fleet appeared offshore from out of the drifting mists, with the bright morning light behind it, and opened fire on the English ships in Sole Bay. In all likelihood the people of Southwold hurried out of the town as soon as the first cannonades were fired to watch the rare spectacle from the beach. Shading their eyes with their hands against the dazzling sun, they would have watched the ships moving hither and thither, apparently at random, their sails billowing in a light northeast wind and then, as they manoeuvred ponderously, flapping once again. They would not have been able to make out human figures at that distance, not even the gentlemen of the Dutch and English admiralties on the bridges. As the battle continued, the powder magazines exploded, and some of the tarred hulls burned down to the waterline; the scene would have been shrouded in an acrid, yellowish-black smoke creeping across the entire bay and masking the combat from view. While most of the accounts of the battles fought on the so-called fields of honour have from time immemorial been unreliable, the pictorial representations of great naval engagements are without exception figments of the imagination. (76)

Sebald's prose is difficult to excerpt; I have already strained the limits of readerly sympathy, I suspect, by quoting so extensively, and yet the passage continues for several pages longer, its juxtapositions and swerves inseparable from the content of what it treats. Several pages later, still looking out over the same scene, the narrator reflects upon a cloudbank that reminds him of a mountain range he once walked the length of (it seemed a thousand miles long) in a dream:

The jagged peaks of the mountains I had left behind rose in almost fearful silhouette against a turquoise sky in which two or three pink clouds drifted. It was a scene that felt familiar in an explicable way, and for weeks it was on my mind until at length I realized that, down to the last detail, it matched the Vallüla massif, which I had seen from the bus, through eyes drooping with tiredness, a day or so before I started school, as we returned home from an outing to the Montafon. I suppose it is submerged memories that give to dreams their curious air of hyper-reality. But perhaps there is something else as well, something nebulous, gauze-like, through which everything one sees in a dream seems, paradoxically, much clearer. A pond becomes a lake, a breeze becomes a storm, a handful of dust is a desert, a grain of sulphur in the blood is a volcanic inferno. What manner of theatre is it, in which we are at once playwright and actor, stage manager, scene painter and audience? (79–80)

The use of small elements to invoke the large is near-magical, the kind of sympathetic magic that works by metaphor and metonymy (the use of a puddle of water, a few twigs, a scrap of sailcloth and the human breath, for instance, to solicit beneficial winds for a ship at sea); the cumulative effect owes something to Proust, undoubtedly, but there is no such clear end goal here as in Proust's recreation of the lost past.

Sebald's narrator is preoccupied with impossible viewing points: the bird's-eye view of the vantage point of Jacob van Ruisdael's *View of Haarlem with Bleaching Fields*, the Waterloo Panorama. The latter is housed "in an immense domed rotunda, where from a raised platform in the middle one can view the battle—a favorite with panorama artists—in every direction."

It is like being at the center of events. On a sort of landscaped proscenium, immediately below the wooden rail amidst tree-stumps and undergrowth in the blood-stained sand, lie lifesize horses, and cut-down infantrymen, hussars and chevaux-légers, eyes rolling in pain or already extinguished. Their faces are moulded from wax but the boots, the leather belts, the weapons, the cuirasses, and the splendidly coloured uniforms, probably stuffed with eelgrass, rags and the like, are to all appearances authentic. Across this horrific three-dimensional scene, on which the cold dust of time has settled, one's gaze is drawn to the horizon, to the enormous mural, one hundred and

ten yards by twelve, painted in 1912 by the French marine
artist Louis Dumontin on the inner wall of the circus-
like structure. This then, I thought, as I looked round
about me, is the representation of history. It requires a
falsification of perspective. We, the survivors, see everything from above, see everything at once, and still we
do not know how it was. The desolate field extends all
around where once fifty thousand soldiers and ten thousand horses met their end within a few hours. The night
after the battle, the air must have been filled with death
rattles and groans. Now there is nothing but the silent
brown soil. Whatever became of the corpses and mortal
remains? Are they buried under the memorial? Are we
standing on a mountain of death? Is that our ultimate
vantage point? Does one really have the much-vaunted
historical overview from such a position? Near Brighton,
I was once told, not far from the coast, there are two
copses that were planted after the Battle of Waterloo in
remembrance of that memorable victory. One is in the
shape of a Napoleonic three-cornered hat, the other in
that of a Wellington boot. Naturally the outlines cannot be made out from the ground; they were intended as
landmarks for latter-day balloonists. (124–25)

At one point the book gives us a little glimpse of Lear and
the dead Cordelia, "both of them so tiny, as if on a stage a mile
off" (174), words that highlight the similar effects of viewing
technologies and theater itself, and the reader is repeatedly
asked to attend to miniature things and models, not just the
ones I have already mentioned but a host of others, including one of my favorites, which comes in a meditation on the
intimacy between the history of art and the history of sugar.
The connection is expressed in the fact that families traf-
ficking in sugar lavished their profits on country residences

and town houses full of art, and many important museums were endowed by sugar dynasties or connected in one way or another with the sugar trade, with trade money legitimized by this sort of patronage:

> At times it seems to me, said [Cornelis] de Jong, as if all works of art were coated with a sugar glaze or indeed made completely of sugar, like the model of the battle of Esztergorn created by a confectioner to the Viennese court, which Empress Maria Theresia, so it is said, devoured in one of her recurrent bouts of melancholy. (194)

The characters who populate the pages of Sebald's book are themselves afflicted with all sorts of melancholy compulsions that speak to their being immured in a lost past: the poet Edward FitzGerald has an endless passion for the correspondence of Madame de Sévigné, who is "far more real to him than even his friends who were still alive," which prompts him to assemble a massive and never-to-be-completed dictionary "which would not only provide commentary on all her correspondents and all the persons and places referred to in their exchanges but would also offer a key of sorts to the way in which she had cultivated and developed the art of writing" (200); the secluded lives, on a remote Irish estate, of the Ashbury family, who live "like refugees who have come through dreadful ordeals and do not now dare to settle in the place where they have ended up" and whose members occupy themselves with work that "always had about it something aimless and meaningless . . . not so much part of a daily routine as an expression of a deeply engrained distress" (a son working for fifteen years on a ten-yard fat-bellied boat, though he knows nothing about boat-building, or a mother collecting flower seeds in paper bags which hang under the library ceiling like clouds of paper [210–22]). One of the most memorable of these figures concerns the farmer Thomas Abrams, who has been toiling for twenty years on a perfect scale model of the Temple of Jerusalem, its completion endlessly deferred due "to the size of the model, which covers nearly ten square yards, and to the minuteness and precision of the individual pieces" (243), a project that seems (even to its creator) in equal parts meticulous and futile.

The icon for the book itself is Sir Thomas Browne's figure of the *quincunx*, the netlike geometric pattern echoed in all sorts of other figures here, from the "invisible net" of the radar that protected British airspace during World War II (227) to the warp and weft of eighteenth-century domestic silk manufacture. Sebald's net-like structure involves the stitching together of one bit to another so that the strands cannot really be disentangled. This loose and unorthodox patterning is somewhat akin to the kinds of unconventional ordering principle that attracted Perec, Barthes and others— alphabetical organization, other experimental ordering of one kind or another, the nonnarrative sequential ordering of Koestenbaum's "My '80s" and Sante's "Commerce"—and it may be said that style, insofar as it foregrounds the unit of the sentence, has an affinity with the nonnarrative.

Many of the fiction writers whose sentences and undertakings are most interesting to me (Lydia Davis, David Markson, Thomas Bernhard) are working in a format that is significantly less oriented toward narrative than most other fiction. That is not to say that style is incompatible with narrative. On the contrary: novels by Austen, Flaubert and others represent the supple and dynamic knitting together of the sentence-oriented sharpness of the aphorism with a forward propulsion that depends on story, plot, mystery, fate in a fashion that is deeply embedded in chronological time and that relies on the development of plot and character and all of the other traditional components of the genre we call the novel. As Sebald represents in many ways a culmination of what can be done with the wayward wandering Proustian first-person voice, wandering in time and place, so Hollinghurst can be seen as at once a striking traditionalist and an extraordinary innovator in the line of descent that runs from Austen and Flaubert through to Henry James. Though his novels look much like the great works of nineteenth-century fiction, in other words, Hollinghurst's style seems to me no less innovative than the more obviously estranging techniques practiced by Perec or Sebald, and this is not just because he includes the transgressive subject matter of men having sex with men and taking drugs: it has to do with the sentences he writes and what he believes they can do.

The Line of Beauty's protagonist, Nick Guest, is writing his thesis on James and calls himself a Jamesian. James is present by allusion within the narrative, and present on almost every page in terms of the homage paid to his narrative voice and use of point of view. *The Golden Bowl* is particularly strong here as an influence, not just in the novel's preoccupation with beautiful objects, their worth and their flaws but in the treatment of important questions about knowledge and perspective in a format that gives the power of filtering everything to the consciousness of an individual character. Hollinghurst hews even more closely and consistently to Nick's point of view, though, than James does to those of the Prince and Maggie. I will quote the novel's opening paragraph in full—the novel is broken into three sections, each with a title and a date: "The Love-Chord" (1983), "To Whom Do You Beautifully Belong?" (1986) and "The End of the Street" (1987):

Peter Crowther's book on the election was already in the shops. It was called *Landslide!*, and the witty assistant at Dillon's had arranged the window in a scaled-down version of that natural disaster. The pale-gilt image of the triumphant Prime Minister rushed towards the customer in a gleaming slippage. Nick stopped in the street, and then went in to look at a copy. He had met Peter Crowther once, and heard him described as a hack and also as a "mordant analyst": his faint smile, as he flicked through the pages, concealed his uncertainty as to which account was nearer the truth. There was clearly something hacklike in the speed of publication, only two months after the event; and in the actual writing, of course. The book's mordancy seemed to be reserved for the efforts of the Opposition. Nick looked carefully at the photographs, but only one of them had Gerald in it: a group picture of "The 101 New Tory MPs," in which he'd been clever enough, or quick enough, to get into the front row. He sat there smiling and staring as if in his own mind it was already the front bench. The smile, the white collar worn with a dark shirt, the floppy breast-pocket handkerchief would surely be famous when the chaps in the rows behind were mere forgotten grins and frowns. Even so, he was mentioned only twice in the text—as a "bon viveur," and as one of the "dwindling minority" of Conservative MPs who had passed, "as Gerald Fedden, the new Member for Barwick, so obviously has," through public school and Oxbridge. Nick left the shop with a shrug; but out in the street he felt delayed pride at this sighting of a person he knew in a published book. (3)

The third-person voice here is an immensely precise tool for registering degrees of knowledge and incomprehension. Nick is hypersensitive to social nuance but inexperienced enough to have only a precarious grasp on the meanings of what he sees; he is a class outsider in this world of privilege, which makes him at once acutely observant and uncertain in his judgments. Though the voice remains very close to Nick's own point of view, in other words, the novelist is able to hint at things that Nick himself does not understand, including (in the title and the shop display) the hint that the election of Margaret Thatcher will indeed have been a natural disaster of sorts for many, though not for all of the characters whose lives this novel will chronicle. Nick has an ear for satire but as yet lacks the confidence in his own judgment to position himself as a satirist, though his emerging self confidence can be heard in the aphorisms that puncture the description. The narrator notes Nick's "faint smile" and the uncertainty it conceals, but the following sentence is sharper and more confident, and it seems to emerge from Nick's consciousness rather than exclusively pertaining to the narrator's voice: "The book's mordancy seemed to be reserved for the efforts of the Opposition." It is the sort of remark one might utter to get a laugh at a certain kind of dinner party: Nick has been studying the ways of the set he's now moving among, and has begun to be able to capture a style of wit that will qualify him to socialize there even as he remains an outsider with only a temporary passport to belonging. Nick takes a childish pleasure in his proximity to the minor players of the Thatcher revolution as singled out by this ephemeral political chronicle, and the effect of the passage as a whole is to underline Nick's failure to understand anything of the significance of the historical moment he's living through.

Nick went to university with Gerald Fedden's son Toby, and is now a tenant in the Feddens' London house with a mandate to keep an eye out for Toby's psychologically frail younger sister, Catherine. His position as a visitor (enshrined, too, in his surname) conditions his behavior as well as his perceptions:

As an outsider he found himself floating again in a pleasant medium of social charm and good humour. Toby and Catherine could frown and sulk, and exercise their prerogative not to be impressed or amused by their parents. Nick, though, conversed with his hosts in an idiom of tremendous agreement. "Did you have glorious weather?" "I must say we had *glorious* weather." "I hope the traffic wasn't too frightful . . ." "*Frightful!*" "I'd love to see the little church at Podier." "I think you'd *love* the little church at Podier." So they knitted their talk together. Even disagreements, for instance over Gerald's taste for Richard Strauss, had a glow of social harmony to them, of relished licence, and counted almost as agreements transposed into a more exciting key. (20–21)

There is a sharp satirical edge to the prose here; Nick's agreement verges on parody as he echoes an idiom not yet quite natural to him, and the final sentence has the air of aphoristic summing-up (the metaphor of the transposition of keys can be imagined to have drifted into the third-person narration via Nick's aesthete's consciousness). Hollinghurst cunningly offers us some emblems for the place of satire in his narrative technique; two caricatures of Gerald Fedden hang on the kitchen wall, drawings "which he had made a point of buying from the cartoonists": "When Gerald was in the kitchen, guests always found themselves contrasting him with his grinning, hawk-nosed cartoon image; the comparison was obviously to his advantage, though it couldn't help stirring the suspicion that under his handsome everyday mask this predatory goon might indeed be lurking" (19–20). Note the compactness and power of this style of notation, the economy with which the words register something about Gerald and the way those around him perceive him and the political and social media in which he operates, not to mention Nick's own funny combination of the obtuse and the perceptive, his cautious trying-out (always filtered through that highly polished and accomplished and self-contained third-person voice) of modes of commentary in which he is still a novice.

Another passage, part of the description of Nick's first date with Leo, foregrounds the centrality of scrutiny, of ways of knowing in this novel. Here is the intensity of perception of a twenty-year-old to whom everything is new, whose capacities to observe and comprehend are great but who is still, as it were, trying out various social affects (again, the third-person voice is extremely close but not identical to Nick's point of view):

> Leo was certainly quite an egotist—Catherine's graphological analysis had been spot on. But he didn't expound his inner feelings. He did something Nick couldn't imagine doing himself, which was to make statements about the sort of person he was. "I'm the sort of guy who needs a lot of sex," he said, and, "I'm like that, I always say what I think." Nick wondered for a moment if he'd inadvertently contradicted him. "I don't bear grudges," Leo said sternly: "I'm not that kind of person." "I'm sure you're not," Nick said, with a quick discountenancing shudder. And perhaps this was a useful skill, or tactic, in the blind-date world, even if Nick's modesty and natural fastidiousness kept him from replying in the same style ("I'm the sort of guy who likes Pope more than Wordsworth," "I'm crazy about sex but I haven't had it yet"). (30)

It is self-deprecating, even self-mocking of Nick to suggest that the meanings of the statement "I'm the sort of guy who likes Pope more than Wordsworth" would be immediately legible to his contemporaries, but in fact that particular preference is a time-honored way of marking out one's own aesthetic and (by extension) sociocultural affiliations. Many of the poets of British Romanticism, Wordsworth foremost among them, dismissed Alexander Pope's poetry as miniaturizing, concerned only with the reproduction of trifling domestic interiors, as opposed to the more masculine pleasures to be found in a poetry of the open air. Lord Byron set himself apart from this consensus and expressed a dandyish celebration of Pope's artifice, and the whole thing would go down in literary history under the name of the Pope controversy.[2]

The high-cultural frame of reference matters a great deal in this novel, and unpacking some of the book's allusions further illuminates the extraordinary craftiness of Hollinghurst's technique. The Feddens with Nick as appendage travel down to Toby's uncle's estate in the country for a lavish twenty-first-birthday party, and traffic threatens to make them late for lunch, provoking an anxiety that Rachel Fedden attempts to diffuse by suggesting that her brother won't mind as they're just "taking pot luck" (43):

Pot luck turned out to be an exquisite light lunch served at a round table in a room lined with rococo *boiseries* that had been removed wholesale from some grand Parisian town house, and painted pale blue. On the ceiling, in a flowered ellipse, two naked females held a wreath of roses. Nick saw at once that the landscape over the fireplace was a Cézanne. It gave him a hilarious sense of his own social displacement. It was one of those moments that only the rich could create, and which came for Nick all wrapped up in its own description, so that he was already recounting it to some impressionable other person—a person, that is, as impressionable as himself. He didn't know whether he should refer to it, but Lord Kessler said as he sat down, "You see I've moved that Cézanne." (45)

Nick is alienated from others of his generation by his aesthete's vocabulary and frame of reference; the depth and breadth of his knowledge are partly explained within the novel by the fact of his father's being an antique dealer, giving it something of the smell of the shop, but Nick has also sharpened his aesthetic sense into an exceptional tool. The vocabulary here is Nick's as well as the narrator's ("rococo *boiseries*"), and the choice of Cézanne is clever: in one sense, the name simply stands for a whole class of paintings that most of us will only ever encounter in public museums rather than private homes, but Cézanne is also *the* name to conjure with when it comes to questions of realism and representation, so that it's a small joke about the history of representation for Hollinghurst to have chosen this particular painter rather than, say, Monet or Matisse.

The furniture at Hawkeswood is "mostly French, and of astonishing quality": Nick straggles behind the others as they walk through the house, his heart beating "with knowledge and suspicion" (the language foregrounds the erotic aspect of this sort of aesthetic apprehension). The particular piece of furniture he contemplates here is a Louis Quinze escritoire or writing desk which Lord Kessler tells him was made for Madame de Pompadour, and the tone of the narration captures Nick's own breathless appreciation and his simultaneous skepticism about whether these objects are sufficiently appreciated by those who live with them. Nick stands with Lord Kessler to admire "the bulbous, oddly diminutive desk—kingwood, was it?—with fronds of ormolu" (here the narration directly registers the deferential and yet authoritative tone of Nick's manner), but the thought registered in the prose upon Nick's arrival in the library is more sardonic:

Lord Kessler himself took him off to the library, where the books were apparently less important than their bindings, which were as important as could be. The heavy gilding of the spines, seen through the fine gilt grilles of the carved and gilded bookcases, created a mood of minatory opulence. They seemed to be books in some quite different sense from those that Nick used and handled every day. (47)

Is it the narrator or Nick himself who is the budding aphorist capable of formulating that verdict about the books' bindings, "as important as could be"? It is not the sort of question that can be answered, but insofar as there is an answer, it must be *both*, just as the phrase "minatory opulence" may well be Nick's, though we only have access to it through the third-person narration.

Nick is about to begin graduate work in English at University College London, and when Lord Kessler asks him what he has chosen as his field, Nick invokes the term *style* itself:

"I want to have a look at *style*," Nick said. This flashing emphasis on something surely ubiquitous had impressed the admissions board, though Lord Kessler appeared uncertain. A man who owned Mme de Pompadour's escritoire could hardly be indifferent to style, Nick felt; but his reply seemed to have in mind some old wisdom about style and substance. (49)

One drama that plays out in the novel concerns the question of whether Nick's faith in style can possibly be borne out, whether style can carry the weight he wants it to (in the absence of any clear set of ethical or political commitments, style is all Nick's got). Nick is in many respects an unsympathetic character, immature, self-absorbed and painfully ignorant of what's at stake in the political developments of these early years of his adulthood. But his knowledge of and love for beautiful things is one of the few true things about him. In the "ongoing Strauss feud" conducted between Nick and Gerald, it becomes "urgent for [Nick] to revile Richard Strauss," which he does "happily but a little hysterically, as if far more than questions of taste were involved" (86). The radio commentator on the Saturday morning program to which Nick and Gerald are listening here (the "Building a Library" feature on BBC Radio 3) points to Strauss's self-glorifying allusions, in his later work, to his own earlier output; Gerald responds viscerally and warmly to the same quality in Strauss that strikes Nick as "bumptious self-confidence" (85). The announcer (a "clever young man," in the narrator's sly phrasing) suggests of a particular recording that "the sheer opulence of the sound and those very broad tempi [might] push this reading over the edge, losing that essential drop of self-irony without which the piece can all too easily become an orgy of vulgarity" (86): a concept that Gerald is virtually incapable of understanding but that is related to Nick's distaste. Catherine likes Strauss even less than Nick does but lacks his precise vocabulary for lambasting it; she simply calls Strauss and all other heavily orchestrated Romantic music "God-dammery," a term explicated by the third-person narrator in terms native to Nick's intellect and imagination:

What the problem was was this colossal redundancy, the squandering of brilliant technique on cheap material, the sense that the moral nerves had been cut, leaving the great bloated body to a life of valueless excess. And then there was the sheer bad taste of applying the high metaphysical language of Wagner to the banalities of bourgeois life, an absurdity Strauss seemed only intermittently aware of! But he couldn't say that, he would sound priggish, he would seem to care too much. Gerald would say it was only music. Nick tried to read the paper for a couple of minutes, but was oddly too excited to concentrate. (87)

Extraordinarily perceptive and articulate in his aesthetic responses, Nick is obtuse in his political ignorance, though the narrator in this respect clearly has a wider knowledge, a perspective on the Thatcher years of which young Nick could have no inkling and to which older Nick may only hope to aspire. I am interested in the stylistic implications of this gap in knowledge; Nick is narratorial, as it were, in his perceptiveness and phrasing and observations, and the local effects of each paragraph owe a great deal to his filtering or framing consciousness, but he is also closed off from kinds of knowledge the narrator may have available to him. (It is only a potentiality at this early point in the novel.) Hollinghurst's touch is very lovely in his weaving of Nick's own phrases into the third-person narration. Consider this description of Leo, for instance: "He was wearing the same old jeans of their first date, which for Nick now had a touching anecdotal quality, he knew them and loved them; and a zipped-up tracksuit top which made him look ready for action, or for inaction, the rigours and hanging about of training" (91). The application of the phrase "anecdotal quality" is Nick's wittiness, not just the narrator's (this is marked partly, I think, in Hollinghurst's choice of how to punctuate the sentence, with the associative comma chosen in preference to the perhaps more correct semicolon that could have preceded the clause "he knew them and loved them"), and we are attracted to Nick, despite his evident flaws and weaknesses, partly because of these powers of perception and description, powers that are also what draw us to the narrative voice. Nick can trust to nothing but this set of skills and a deeply founded set of aesthetic precepts, and his moments of misunderstanding and panic around others often hinge on questions of artistic (mis)interpretation. It is the discussion, at cross-purposes, of the Holman Hunt painting whose reproduction hangs in Leo's mother's house ("just the sort of painting, doggedly literal and morbidly symbolic, that Nick liked least" [141]) that shows the impossibility of Nick's coexisting with Leo's family members, and when Nick tells Leo that his mother and sister are "wonderful," he hears "the word hang, in the silence between the lights, as if in inverted commas, and underlined too: the wonderful of gush, of connoisseurship, of Kensington Park Gardens" (144). In the end, he is not sundered from Leo by the fact of his response to *Scarface* (to Nick, shocking, bombastic) in the scene that follows—they have gone to the film on Leo's recommendation, but Leo doesn't like it much either. In the moment before he learns this, though, Nick "as so often [has] the feeling that an artistic disagreement, almost immaterial to the other person, was going to be the vehicle of something that mattered to him more than he could say" (148).

The second part of *The Line of Beauty* is set in 1986, the third in 1987, and each one represents the further corrosion of Nick's painful innocence, his entrance into a world of knowledge. Nick is now the lover of the glamorous English-Lebanese playboy Wani, and his induction into a more sophisticated and corrupt sexuality than the one Leo facilitated in the first part of the book is one of the forms of knowledge that continues to push Nick's perspective into even closer alignment with that of the knowing narrator. The subtlety of the play between those two perspectives, mostly overlapping and sometimes abruptly—briefly—sundered, is astonishing. Nick lives with Wani in the flat on the top two floors of a Kensington house whose ground floor houses the magazine offices for *Ogee*, the magazine named for the eighteenth-century artist William Hogarth's "line of beauty," an S-shaped curve that Hogarth believed would impart liveliness to any composition:

Nick smiled to himself at the flat's pretensions, but inhabited it with his old wistful keenness, as he did the Feddens' house, as a fantasy of prosperity that he could share, and as the habitat of a man he was in love with. He felt he took to it well, the comfort and convenience, the discreet glimpsed world of things that the rich had done for them. It was a system of minimized stress, of guaranteed flattery. Nick loved the huge understanding depth of the sofas and the peculiarly gilding light of the lamps that flanked the bathroom basin; he had never looked so well as he did when he shaved or cleaned his teeth there. Of course the house was vulgar, as almost everything postmodern was, but he found himself taking a surprising pleasure in it. (175)

It is a knife's edge only that separates Nick's knowledge from the narrator's. It is impossible to say for sure where Nick's knowledge ends: does Nick himself have access to the phrase "his old wistful keenness," and to the psychological insight implied in it? To the sort of self-distancing implied not just in the ability to think "I have taken to it well" but to phrase it, instead, "I feel I have taken to it well"? And is such attentiveness to phrasing a matter of intelligence and insight, or merely of fussiness? Perhaps the clearest marker of Nick's passage through time is his new comfort with vulgarity: he is no longer so trammeled by the fastidious tastes of his upbringing.

Nick's affair with Wani is a secret from the magazine's other employees, to whom Nick manages to present himself as a wise sophisticate. One of his favorite conversational techniques is to utter phrases adapted from Henry James: "a trifle too punctually, though not yet quite lamentably bald"; "he spoke, as to cheek and chin, of the joy of the matutinal steel" (182). Nick "felt he was prostituting the Master," the narrative continues, "but then there was an element of self-mockery in these turns of phrase—it was something he was looking at in his thesis. He was at the height of a youthful affair with his writer, in love with his rhythms, his ironies, and his idiosyncrasies, and loving his most idiosyncratic moments most of all" (182–83).

"Youthful" must be strictly the narrator's term, not Nick's—it is near-inconceivable that Nick could in this context apply the adjective to himself—but that perspective offers a sense of the precariousness of Nick's fantastic current life. Hollinghurst alludes to James repeatedly, as when Nick reads James's memoir by the swimming pool at the Feddens' place in France:

> He was reading Henry James's memoir of his childhood, *A Small Boy and Others*, and feeling crazily horny, after three days without as much as a peck from Wani. It was a hopeless combination. The book showed James at his most elderly and elusive, and demanded a pure commitment unlikely in a reader who was worrying excitedly about his boyfriend and semi-spying, through dark glasses, on another boy who was showing off in front of him and clearly trying to excite him. From time to time the book tilted and wobbled in his lap, and the weight of the deckle-edged pages pressed on his erection through the sleek black nylon. He noted droll phrases for later use: "an oblong farinaceous compound" was James's euphemism for a waffle—*compound* was sublime in its clinching vagueness. (273)

The contrast between Nick's sexual arousal and his reading of James is shocking, but it is partially domesticated by the extent to which the juxtaposition is managed by Nick himself for maximum titillation, with the phrase "deckle-edged pages" itself suggesting a certain level of self-mockery (deckle edges are the rough and uneven trim on books from an era when the pages still had to be cut with a knife, though they continue to appear on mass-produced books to tastelessly ornamental ends).

It is almost clinical, the dispassion with which the narrator notes Nick's slightly embarrassing mining of James's pages for witty remarks of the sort we have already seen him using with his coworkers in the office. Nick's only sincerity lies in his love of beautiful things, but his reliance on that love is shaken or swayed by the temptations of adult life. The narrator observes, of the market hall in the town where Nick grew up (it is also Gerald's constituency, and Nick has returned for the election):

> It had been the pride of Nick's childhood, he had done a project about it at school with measured plans and elevations, at the age of twelve it had ranked with the Taj Mahal and the Parliament Building in Ottawa in his private architectural heaven. The moment of accepting that it was not by Wren had been as bleak and exciting as puberty. (249)

The distance between young Nick and older Nick is painful; young Nick's unselfconscious love for architecture (the fact that he *has* such a thing as a private architectural heaven, and the appealing nerdiness of the triumvirate of buildings Hollinghurst selects for it) endears him to us, but only at the risk of mild ridicule, and the simile of the second sentence highlights the grotesque aspect of this strong identification rather than its seductive one. Most people (though not, presumably, most people who like Hollinghurst's novels) would find it ludicrous to compare the passing into knowledge that represents giving up the fantasy of one's local favorite building having been designed by the great architect to whom it is commonly attributed with the transfigurations of puberty, described here with a pair of adjectives that is lovely precisely because the words' mating is so deeply unexpected.

Nick's love for beautiful things is associated here with his sexuality; the novel plays around with the idea that all male aesthetes must be gay (witness Nick's earlier speculations about the man who owns Madame de Pompadour's escritoire), and it is observed of Toby's sandwich-making that "it was a bit of a mess, a mishmash, lots of dressing was sploshed in—it was almost as though he was saying to Nick, who had once had a job in a sandwich shop, 'I'm not a poof, I haven't got style, I can't help it'" (280). Part 2 of the novel culminates in the celebratory party at the Fedden house at which Margaret Thatcher (referred to here only as "the Lady") makes her appearance. Nick, in a haze of cocaine-induced confidence, is the only man bold enough to present himself as a partner:

> He gazed delightedly at the Prime Minister's face, at her whole head, beaked and crowned, which he saw was a fine if improbable fusion of the Vorticist and the Baroque. She smiled back with a certain animal quickness, a bright blue challenge. There was the soft glare of the flash—twice—three times—a gleaming sense of occasion, the gleam floating in the eye as a blot of shadow, his heart running fast with no particular need of courage as he grinned and said, "Prime Minister, would you like to dance?" (335)

It is almost one of Nick's Jamesisms, this affected but sharp analysis of Thatcher's appearance as "a fine if improbable fusion of the Vorticist and the Baroque" (we feel Nick's own enjoyment in the sharp unexpectedness of the insight and the pungency of his own phrasing), and the tableau is one of the most vivid scenes in the book.

Despite the pseudo-sophistication of this Nick, there is a terrible naïveté in the pleasure he takes in his new world of money and cocaine and unlimited sex. Indeed, he is still considerably less worldly-wise than he understands himself to be, a fact revealed by his shock at the discovery of an affair between Gerald Fedden and his secretary, Penny. One way of describing the central drama of the book as a whole—certainly of its last section—is to say that it asks whether art can really be the repository of morality in the way that Nick would like to believe, or whether it will prove insufficient to the burdens of ethics and politics. That final section is considerably shorter than the two preceding ones and quite different in tone; it takes an unexpected swerve, and calls much of what we have come to take for granted about the novel's aestheticism into question. We learn that Leo has died of AIDS, and Wani will soon do so (his beauty has been devastated—"He commanded attention now by pity and respect as he once had by beauty and charm. . . . Nick thought he still looked wonderful in a way, though to admit it was to make an unbearable comparison. He was twenty-five years old" [376]). The precedent of Henry James looms very large still here, but Nick's adherence to a Jamesian style has come to seem increasingly irrelevant—almost self-delusional—in the context of Wani's illness, Leo's death and the scandal that's about to break when news of Gerald's affair gets out.

As I mentioned earlier, one aspect of James's "late" style, those long winding sentences of infinite syntactical complexity, is commonly attributed to James's having adopted the habit of dictating rather than writing by hand; Nick, too, dictates letters to his secretary, and finds himself like James "able to improvise long supple sentences rich in suggestions and syntactic shock," all "old-fashioned periods and perplexing semi-colons" (346). This is "periods" in the sense of *oratori-cal* periods, those sentences structured with a Ciceronian balance redolent of the eighteenth century ("I sighed as a lover, I obeyed as a son"). But the power of aestheticism to ward off the sordid has worn very thin, and an objective correlative for the sorts of moral decay expressed in political and sexual corruption can be found in the formerly lovely desk in Wani's house: "The Georgian desk was marked with drink stains and razor etchings that even the optimistic Don Guest would have found it hard to disguise. 'That's beyond cosmetic repair, old boy,' Don would say. Nick fingered at the little abrasions and found himself gasping and whooping with grief" (357).

It is the news of Leo's death that has exposed the tawdriness and pretension of Wani's flat to Nick, so that he can express his emotional wretchedness only by mourning (on the face of it) the destruction of a beautiful object, an object no less thoroughly ruined by the excesses of the previous years than Leo and Wani have both been. But it is in this scene that Nick finds some measure of redemption, the return to a simpler aestheticism (or at any rate a form of emotion still experienced primarily through objects but not necessarily culpable just because it represents a displacement from the human) that gives him at least the first inklings of ethical awareness. It is "an anxious refinement of tact" that makes him uncomfortable even mentioning Leo's death in the condolence letter he writes to Leo's mother:

"Your sad news," "recent sad events" . . . : "Leo's death" was brutal. Then he worried that "I was so terribly sorry" might sound like gush to her, like calling her wonderful. He knew his own forms of truth could look like insincerity to others. He was frightened of her, as a grieving woman, and uncertain what feelings to attribute to her. It seemed she had taken it all in her own way, perhaps even with a touch of zealous cheerfulness. He could see her being impressed by his educated form of words and best handwriting. Then he saw her looking mistrustfully at what he'd written. He felt the limits of connoisseurship of tone. It was what he was working on, and yet. . . . He stared out of the window, and after a minute found Henry James's phrase about the death of Poe peering back at him. What was it? *The extremity of personal absence had just overtaken him.* The words, which once sounded arch and even facetious, were suddenly terrible to him, capacious, wise, and hard. He understood for the first time that they'd been written by someone whose life had been walked through, time and again, by death. And then he saw himself, in six months' time perhaps, sitting down to write a similar letter to the denizens of Lowndes Square. (358)

The denizens of Lowndes Square are Wani's family members, and the revelation that hits Nick here is like something out of a Greek tragedy.

His encounter with the physical artifact of the magazine, its first and only issue, which arrives in a bundle from the printers near the end of the novel casts another light on the relationship between aesthetics and ethics:

Strange teetering mood of culmination. Five minutes later he wished he had it to read through fresh again; but that could never happen. He took a copy upstairs to the flat, and opened it at random several times—to find that its splendour had a glint to it, a glassy malignity. No, it was very good. It was lustrous. The lustre was perfected and intense—it was the shine of marble and varnish. It was the gleam of something that was over. (428)

This is one of a cluster of passages that reflect on the relationship between beauty, style and the emotions, as in the scene where Nick (the revelation of his scandalous activities during his time as a lodger at the Feddens having lost him his place there) realizes he must tell Gerald that he will leave the house:

Nick went up to his room, and stood looking at the window sill. Late-morning, late-October sunlight dimmed and brightened indifferently over it. He was lost in thought, but it was thought without words, pure abstraction, luminous and sad. Then a simple form of words appeared, almost as if written. It would have been best in a letter, where it could have been done beautifully, with complete control. Spoken, it risked tremors and deflections. He went downstairs to see Gerald. (415)

The temptation to avoid the risk of being seen to be moved by emotion is presented here with immense humanity and tolerance, even as writing is shown to be a coward's recourse for dodging the "tremors and deflections" of the personal encounter.

10

The Bind of Literature
and the Bind of Life

Voices from Chernobyl,
Thomas Bernhard, Karl Ove Knausgaard

L oss has prompted some of the most lovely writing in the literary tradition (think of the lines in the *Iliad* where Priam
petitions for the return of Hector's body), but it is surely the
desire not to commemorate but to ward off emotional pain,
in a world approaching modernity, that partly precipitated the
rise of free indirect style in the early nineteenth century. This
claim will risk sounding dandyish, overstated, but how else
to explain the role of the impersonal in style as two centuries of novelists have conceived it? It is impossible to ascribe
intimate properties to third-person narrators whose voices
are highly distinctive and yet altogether lacking the sorts of
"traits" possessed by actual people. The distance of an Aus-
tenian or a Flaubertian narrator remains compatible, though,
with the evocation and expression of a range of strong

emotions: embarrassment, shame, self-revelation in the case of Austen, say, a savage sorrow and a kind of disgust at humanity in the case of *Madame Bovary*, self-pity and envy in *The Line of Beauty*. James's fictions often feature the framing or displacement of emotions: *The Golden Bowl* is a story in which nothing much happens except for one thing that is almost incomprehensibly painful (indeed, indescribably so) for the two women most directly concerned in it. In the tradition that runs through Roland Barthes to Susan Sontag and Wayne Koestenbaum, we see a heightened intensity or awareness of perception that has some kind of *charge* to it (often an almost erotic charge) but that deliberately downplays, too, the personal in the sense of the full range of human personality.

In her book *Monomania: The Flight from Everyday Life in Literature and Art*, Marina Van Zuylen suggests that artists like Mondrian and Flaubert, obsessed with

> the relationship of their straight line or perfect phrase to a sense of ontological security, . . . are splitting the world between the rigid (with its connotations of self-discipline, rigor, and control) and the arabesque, the overly lyrical *I*—all things that might well lead them out of their invulnerable worlds. . . . Do not show your passion, but sublimate it into style. We are reminded of Hobbes's proclamation: madness is a matter of "too much appearing passion." It is not the actual emotion itself that is unsettling to Flaubert, but the temptation to be dragged down by it and the sickly need to exhibit it to others. The heart must never speak and the artist must assume a god-like self-sufficiency; it is the only way he will be protected from the danger of others. The same detachment that Flaubert requires of his narrators, he mercilessly exacts from himself. He is willing to renounce all human contact for the price of peace of mind.[1]

Van Zuylen goes on to show that what she calls the "mono-maniacal imagination" very consistently displays this "simultaneous cowering from and craving for the void": "Movement, while it fends off the demons of introspection and provides temporary relief from anxiety, does not satisfy the soul's craving for a higher order; it is a mere temporary solution. Idleness, however, richer in existential possibilities, can breed an intolerable sense of dread."

Much of Perec's writing is motivated by precisely this sort of tension. I think for instance of a passage I have always loved, in Perec's early novella *A Man Asleep:*

It is not that you hate men, why would you hate them? Why would you hate yourself? If only membership of the human race were not accompanied by this insufferable din, if only these few pathetic steps taken into the animal kingdom did not have to be bought at the cost of this perpetual, nauseous dyspepsia of words, projects, great departures! But it is too high a price to pay for opposable thumbs, an erect stature, the incomplete rotation of the head on the shoulders: this cauldron, this furnace, this grill which is life, these thousands of summonses, incitements, warnings, thrills, depressions, this enveloping atmosphere of obligations, this eternal machine for producing, crushing, swallowing up, overcoming obstacles, starting afresh and without respite, this insidious terror which seeks to control every day, every hour of your meagre existence![2]

If Sebald cries out against the destruction wreaked by both sides in World War II and Hollinghurst against the destruction wreaked by AIDS and by Thatcherism, Perec's outcry (like Lear's) protests the fact of the human condition itself. There is nothing sentimental about these sentences, but they are capable of bringing tears to my eyes. The passage might be said to perform something at odds with what it proclaims, by which I mean to say that the sentences are passionate even as they foreswear passion: the wild piling-on of "this cauldron, this furnace, this grill which is life, these thousands . . . " is a litany that becomes perversely almost celebratory even as it damningly outlines the contours of modern despair.

Prose styles might be placed along some imaginary axis from the most baroque or lush to the most stringent or self-denying; my own tastes run more to the latter to the former, though there are always exceptions. Three novels I particularly admire but that would strike many readers as overly bleak, in terms of both content and prose style, are Jenny Diski's *Nothing Natural*, Heather Lewis's *House Rules* and Stephen Elliott's *Happy Baby*. Beautifully written novels are infinitely less likely to be joyful than despairing; Angela Carter's *Wise Children* might be a rare exception, though I suppose the novels of Barbara Trapido (like *Wise Children*, inflected by the rhythms of Shakespearean comedy) might fall under this rubric as well.

I anyway can the much, but it cannot do everything. Svetlana Alexievich makes an unusual observation in the introduction to her staggering nonfiction book *Voices from Chernobyl: The Oral History of a Nuclear Disaster*:

I used to think I could understand everything and express everything. Or almost everything. I remember when I was writing my book about the war in Afghanistan, *Zinky Boys*, I went to Afghanistan and they showed me some of the foreign weapons that had been captured from the Afghan fighters. I was amazed at how perfect their forms were, how perfectly a human thought had been expressed. There was an officer standing next to me and he said, "If someone were to step on this Italian mine that you say is so pretty it looks like a Christmas decoration, there would be nothing left of them but a bucket of meat. You'd have to scrape them off the ground with a spoon." When I sat down to write this, it was the first time I thought, "Is this something I should say?" I had been raised on great Russian literature, I thought you could go very very far, and so I wrote about that meat. But the Zone—it's a separate world, a world within the rest of the world—and it's more powerful than anything literature has to say.[3]

This statement cedes everything to testimony, acts of witnessing, and suggests that the writer's role is to facilitate the production and recording of that testimony rather than to create sentences whose beauty and precision might do justice to the perfection of human ingenuity in a machine that brings death. The degradation of human beings into meat poses an unanswerable challenge to style, even for one raised (as Alexievich suggests) on great literature.

There are a number of ways for artists and critics to respond to that despairing lurking awareness that we are just meat puppets. One is to turn to what Jonathan Lethem, in an essay titled "The Beards" (it was first published in the *New Yorker* and later included in Lethem's collection *The Disappointment Artist*), calls "dripless, squeakless art."[4] As a child, Lethem asks his mother why there are drips on his father's paintings, and she offers the analogy that the paint drips are like the squeak of acoustic guitar strings audible in folksingers' recordings. As an adolescent in the grip of unbearable feelings, and in the years beyond adolescence, Lethem asks works of art "to be both safer than life and fuller, a better family," then plumbs them so deeply that "many perfectly sufficient works of art would become thin, anemic":

This was especially true of anything that assumed a posture of minimalism or perfectionism, or of chilly, intellectual grandeur. Hence my rage at Stanley Kubrick, Don DeLillo, Jean-Luc Godard, and Talking Heads. The artists who'd seemed to promise the most were the ones who'd created art that stirred me while seeming to absent themselves from emotional risk—so these were the ones capable of failing my needs most violently. When I discovered their imperfections, my own hope of absenting myself from emotional risk seemed imperiled. It was as though in their coolness these artists had sensed my oversized needs and turned away, flinched from what I'd asked them to feel on my behalf.

Perec also writes out of this sort of a bind, but perhaps the writer who most clearly kicks against it and occasionally transcends it is Thomas Bernhard. In the short novel *Wittgenstein's Nephew*, describing himself just before he mounts the stage to receive a major Austrian literary prize, the narrator (a distorted version of Bernhard himself) says he "had jotted down a few sentences, amounting to a small philosophical digression, the upshot of which was that man was a wretched creature and death a certainty."⁵ To give this sort of remark as an aside is very funny (it is comically inappropriate for delivery on this sort of occasion, though that fact speaks to the dreadfulness of the occasion rather than to anything inherently nonviable about such philosophical digression in its appropriate contexts), but that does not stop it from being also very seriously meant. Here is an early passage that gives the flavor of Bernhard's unrelenting prose; the whole novel is presented in the form of a single paragraph, or rather the paragraph break has no place in this style of narration. The story chronicles the vicissitudes of the friendship between Bernhard's proxy and his real-life friend Paul Wittgenstein, nephew of the philosopher and scion of the prominent and self-destructive Austrian family:

If I had friends staying with me he would go for walks with us. He was not keen to do so, but was prepared to join us. I do not care for walks either, and have been a reluctant walker all my life. I have always disliked walking, but I am prepared to go for walks with friends, and this makes them think I am a keen walker, for there is an amazing *theatricality* about the way I walk. I am certainly not a keen walker, nor am I a nature lover or a nature expert. But when I am with friends I walk in such a way as to convince them I am a keen walker, a nature lover, and a nature expert. I know nothing about nature. I hate nature, because it is killing me. I live in the country only because the doctors have told me that I must live *in the country* if I want to survive—for no other reason. In fact I love everything except nature, which I find sinister; I have become familiar with the malignity and implacability of nature through the way it has dealt with my own body and soul, and being unable to contemplate the beauties of nature without at the same time contemplating its malignity and implacability, I fear it and avoid it whenever I can. The truth is that I am a city dweller who can at best tolerate nature. It is only with reluctance that I live in the country, which on the whole I find hostile. And naturally Paul too was a city dweller through and through, who, like me, was soon exhausted when surrounded by nature. (53)

It is partly the effect of the lack of paragraph breaks, but the way that each sentence knots itself to the previous one by way of repetition and variation leads to the creation of a dense web of meaning, with the narrator the end of this passage seemingly having gone nowhere at all despite having touched down on the misleading theatricality of his walking style, his hatred for nature and his inability to escape it and the link between himself and Paul Wittgenstein based on their shared sense of nature's malignity. This willingness to circle back around the same topics again and again produces an effect unlike anything I have described so far as the characteristic forms of pacing of novel versus short story. Each "episode" in a novel by Bernhard has the feel at once of a comic set piece and a raw unedited transcription of thought, only the prose is too perfect; the tension between the craft of the sentences (and the shape or momentum of individual stretches of prose) and the repetitive or compulsive quality of the narration gives the narrative its underlying dynamism. Here is another passage that stands out:

I have always hated the Viennese coffeehouses, but I go on visiting them. I have visited them every day, for although I have always hated them—and *because* I have always hated them—I have always suffered from the *Viennese coffeehouse disease.* I have suffered more from this disease than from any other. I frankly have to admit that I still suffer from this disease, which has proved the most intractable of all. The truth is that I have always hated the Viennese coffeehouses because in them I am always confronted with people like myself, and naturally I do not wish to be everlastingly confronted with people like myself, and certainly not in a coffeehouse, where I go to escape from myself. Yet it is here that I find myself confronted with myself and my kind. I find myself insupportable, and even more insupportable is a whole horde of writers and brooders like myself. I avoid literature whenever possible, because whenever possible I avoid myself, and so when I am in Vienna I have to forbid myself to visit the coffeehouses, or at least I have to be careful not to visit a so-called literary coffeehouse *under any circumstances whatever.* However, suffering as I do from the coffeehouse disease, I feel an unremitting compulsion to visit some literary coffeehouse or other, even though everything within me rebels against the idea. The truth is that the more deeply I detest the literary coffeehouses of Vienna, the more strongly I feel compelled to frequent them. Who knows how my life would have developed if I had not met Paul Wittgenstein at the height of the crisis that, but for him, would probably have pitched me headlong into the literary world, the most repellent of all worlds, the world of Viennese writers and their intellectual morass, for at the height of this crisis the obvious course would have been to take the easy way out, to make myself cheap and compliant, to surrender and throw in my lot with the literary fraternity. Paul preserved me from this, since he had always detested the literary coffeehouses. It was thus not without reason, but more or less to save myself, that from one day to the next I stopped frequenting the so-called literary coffeehouses and started going to the Sacher with him—no longer to the Hawelka but to the Ambassador, etc., until eventually the moment came when I could once more *permit* myself to go to the literary coffeehouses, when they no longer had such a deadly effect on me. For the truth is that the literary coffeehouses do have a deadly effect on a writer. (85–87)

I am unsettled by the combination of humor and seriousness here. Are these sentences really funny, or is this intolerable, insupportable? Both must be true at once: "I find myself insupportable, and even more insupportable is a whole horde of writers and brooders like myself"; "I avoid literature whenever possible, because whenever possible I avoid myself ": it is the bind of literature, but also the bind of life, and Bernhard's prose will have to serve as fine consolation.

I recently read a passage that summed up what I, too, see as the highest goal of writing. I have published four novels, but I have become increasingly frustrated with the aspect of fiction that involves making up characters and the things that happen to them; it seems to me fatally artificial, an abuse of my own imaginative powers and an insult to what I see as the underlying purpose of any novel I would write (to examine or anatomize a problem or a situation, in the process transmitting something of a mood or an emotional affect—really I am an intellectual at heart rather than a novelist, but I don't see why the two should finally be at odds with one another). When I came to read it, I found Karl Ove Knausgaard's *My Struggle* just as transfixing as everyone said it would be. These words fall near the end of the first volume and represent a kind of turning point as Knausgaard's own vocation comes into clearer focus:

I was after something. And what I concluded on which reading Adorno, for example, lay not in what I read, but in the perception of myself while I was reading. I was someone who read Adorno! And in this heavy, intricate, detailed, precise language whose aim was to elevate thought ever higher, and where every period was set like a mountaineer's cleat, there was something else, this particular approach to the mood of reality, the shadow of these sentences that could evoke in me a vague desire to use the language with this particular mood on something real, on something living. Not on an argument, but on a lynx, for example, or on a blackbird or a cement mixer. For it was not the case that language cloaked reality in its moods, but vice versa, reality arose from them.[6]

It is not so different, strange to say, from the green peas that Barthes hoped would punctuate the intellectual murmur: a fusion of ideas and things in language that becomes in turn a supremely sensitive instrument of the self, the kind of instrument desired by many of the other writers whose words I have most loved. It has been the purpose of these pages to open up to others some of the ways of reading and writing that have shaped my own reality, delighted and consoled me; and now I will simply step aside, given the impossibility of offering any kind of a proper conclusion, so that we can return to our real lives of reading and writing.

NOTES

1. THE GLIMMER FACTOR: ANTHONY BURGESS'S 99 NOVELS

1. Stephen Burt, *Randall Jarrell and His Age* (New York: Columbia University Press, 2002), 2.

2. LORD LEIGHTON, LIBERACE AND THE ADVANTAGES OF BAD WRITING: HELEN DEWITT, HARRY STEPHEN KEELER, LIONEL SHRIVER, GEORGE ELIOT

1. Helen DeWitt, *The Last Samurai* (New York: Talk Miramax, 2000), 57–58.

2. Lydia Millet, "Alice in Familyland," *Globe and Mail*, September 23, 2006, http://www.theglobeandmail.com/news/arts/alice-in-familyland /article193732/. As I finish the last revisions to these pages, Christian Lorentzen has just published "Poor Rose: Against Alice Munro," *London Review of Books* 35, no. 11 (June 6, 2013): 11–12.

3. I have a strong enough sense of fairness, buttressed by feelings of scholarly responsibility, that after writing these words, I did read the novel in question.

4. The passage is from McDermott's novel *After This*, as quoted in Joan Acocella, "Heaven's Gate," *New Yorker*, September 11, 2006, http:// www.newyorker.com/archive/2006/09/11/060911crbo_books.

5. Otto Penzler, "The Worst Writer in the World," *New York Sun*, December 21, 2005, http://www.nysun.com/arts/worst-writer-in-the-world/24771/.

6. Harry Stephen Keeler, *The Riddle of the Traveling Skull*, ed. Paul Collins (San Francisco: McSweeney's, 2005), 182, 191, 111, 201.
7. Lionel Shriver, *The Post-Birthday World* (London: HarperCollins, 2007), 46. Subsequent quotations are from this edition and are given parenthetically in the text.
8. George Eliot, *Middlemarch*, ed. Rosemary Ashton (1871–1872; reprint, London: Penguin, 1994), II.xx.

3. MOUTHY PLEASURES AND THE PROBLEM OF MOMENTUM: GARY LUTZ, *LOLITA*, LYDIA DAVIS, JONATHAN LETHEM

1. Gary Lutz, "The Sentence Is a Lonely Place," *Believer*, January 2009, http://www.believermag.com/issues/200901/?read=article_lutz.
2. Gary Lutz, "Waking Hours," in *Stories in the Worst Way* (1996; reprint, Providence, RI: 3rd bed, 2006), 8–9.
3. Daniel Long, "An Interview with Gary Lutz," *Fiddleback* 1, no. 5, http://thefiddleback.com/_webapp_4159108/An_Interview_with_Gary_Lutz.
4. Vladimir Nabokov, *Lolita* (1955; reprint, New York: Knopf, 1992), 9.
5. Lydia Davis, "Boring Friends," in *The Collected Stories of Lydia Davis* (New York: Farrar, Straus & Giroux, 2009), 313.
6. Lydia Davis, "Samuel Johnson Is Indignant," in *Collected Stories*, 351.
7. Jonathan Lethem, *The Fortress of Solitude* (2003; reprint, New York: Vintage, 2004), 91. Subsequent quotations are from this edition and are given parenthetically in the text.

4. THE ACOUSTICAL ELEGANCE OF APHORISM: KAFKA, FIELDING, AUSTEN, FLAUBERT

1. Jane Austen, *Emma*, ed. James Kinsley, intro. Adela Pinch (Oxford: Oxford University Press, 2003), I.i.5. Subsequent quotations are from this edition and are given parenthetically in the text.
2. Jonathan Swift, *The Poems of Jonathan Swift*, ed. Harold Williams, 2nd ed., 3 vols. (Oxford: Clarendon, 1958), 2:556. The original reads "Danes l'adversité de nos meilleurs amis nous trouvons quelque chose, qui ne nous deplaist pas."
3. Franz Kafka, *The Zürau Aphorisms of Franz Kafka*, trans. Michael Hofman and Geoffrey Brock (New York: Schocken, 2006), #20, #29, #32.
4. Henry Fielding, *The History of Tom Jones, a Foundling*, ed. Alice Wakely, intro. Tom Keymer (London: Penguin, 2005), I.v.
5. Samuel Johnson, vol. 4 of *The Lives of the Most Eminent English*

Poets; with Critical Observations on their Works, ed. Roger Lonsdale (Oxford: Clarendon, 2006), 3.

6. D. A. Miller, "No One Is Alone," in *Jane Austen, or The Secret of Style* (Princeton, NJ: Princeton University Press, 2003), 31–56. The passage quoted is on 31–32.

7. Gustave Flaubert, *Madame Bovary: Provincial Ways*, trans. Lydia Davis (New York: Viking Penguin, 2010), II.12.167. Here is the text in the original language: "Il s'était tant de fois entendu dire ces choses, qu'elles n'avaient pour lui rien d'original. Emma ressemblait à toutes les maîtresses; et le charme de la nouveauté, peu à peu tombant comme un vêtement, laissait voir à nu l'éternelle monotonie de la passion, qui a toujours les mêmes formes et le même langage. Il ne distinguait pas, cet homme si plein de pratique, la dissemblance des sentiments sous la parité des expressions. Parce que des lèvres libertines ou vénales lui avaient murmuré des phrases pareilles, il ne croyait que faiblement à la candeur de celles-là; on en devait rabattre, pensait-il, les discours exagérés cachant les affections médiocres: comme si la plénitude de l'âme ne débordait pas quelquefois par les métaphores les plus vides, puisque personne, jamais, ne peut donner l'exacte mesure de ses besoins, ni de ses conceptions ni de ses douleurs, et que la parole humaine est comme un chaudron fêlé où nous battons des mélodies à faire danser les ours, quand on voudrait attendrir les étoiles"; *Madame Bovary*, ed. Bernard Ajac (1856; reprint, Paris: Flammarion, 1986), 259.

8. James Wood, *How Fiction Works* (New York: Farrar, Straus & Giroux, 2008), 19.

5. TEMPO, REPETITION AND A TAXONOMY OF PACING:
PETER TEMPLE, NEIL GAIMAN, A. L. KENNEDY, EDWARD P. JONES

1. Peter Temple, *Black Tide* (San Francisco: MacAdam/Cage, 2005), 38.

2. Unlike crime fiction, science fiction is a genre less inherently hospitable to beautiful prose—though there are always exceptions to this sort of generalization—even as it magically inherits the mandate of the novel of ideas, no longer commercially viable if it ever was, but now finding new life in a form that potentially reaches huge audiences: an excellent recent example of bestselling science fiction that is also a first-rate novel of ideas would be Neal Stephenson's *Anathem*.

3. Peter Temple, *The Broken Shore* (2005; reprint, New York: Picador, 2008), 127.

4. Neil Gaiman, *Anansi Boys* (New York: William Morrow/HarperCollins,

2005), 135–36. Subsequent quotations are from this edition and are given parenthetically in the text.

5. Luc Sante, "French Without Tears," *Threepenny Review*, Summer 2004, http://www.threepennyreview.com/samples/sante_su04.html.

6. For more on this, see Jim Dawson, *The Compleat Motherfucker: A History of the Mother of All Dirty Words* (2011), esp. 159; I am indebted to Brian Berger for the reference.

7. Laurence Sterne, *The Life and Opinions of Tristram Shandy, Gentleman* (1759–67), ed. Melvyn New and Joan New, intro. Christopher Ricks (New York: Penguin, 2003), V.xvii.339. The missing letters are c h a m b e r p o t and p i s s o u t o f t h e w i n d o w.

8. A. L. Kennedy, *Paradise* (2004; reprint, New York: Random House/ Vintage, 2006), 198.

9. Tobias Hill, "School Stories," *Guardian*, April 5, 2007, http://www .guardian.co.uk/books/2007/apr/05/extract.

10. William Boyd, "The Things I Stole," *Guardian*, August 1, 2008, http:// www.guardian.co.uk/books/2008/aug/02/william.boyd.short.story.

11. Jenny Davidson, "Great Jones," *Village Voice*, August 26, 2006, http:// www.villagevoice.com/2006-08-29/books/great-jones/.

12. Edward P. Jones, *All Aunt Hagar's Children* (New York: HarperCollins/ Amistad, 2006), 395, 237.

7. DISORDERED SENTENCES: GEORGES PEREC, ROLAND BARTHES, WAYNE KOESTENBAUM, LUC SANTE

1. In an affectionate nod to Brent Buckner, I also note the possible congruence between the Myers-Briggs personality types and the Gygaxian system of alignment for AD&D.

2. Roman Jakobson, "Two Aspects of Language and Two Types of Aphasic Disturbances," in *Language in Literature*, ed. Krystyna Pomorska and Stephen Rudy (Cambridge, MA: Belknap/Harvard University Press, 1987), 95–114.

3. Georges Perec, *La disparition* (Paris: Les lettres nouvelles, 1969), 17; and Georges Perec, *A Void*, trans. Gilbert Adair (London: Harvill, 1994), 3.

4. David Bellos explains that Perec was allowed to "cheat" slightly, obtaining permission from his OuLiPo colleagues to make one change to French spelling and a handful of further modifications as needed. The English analogue is that "'and' may be spelt 'n'"; the consonantal "y" is permitted, and so are other distortions of conventional spelling. Georges Perec, *The Exeter Text*, in *Three By Perec*, trans. Ian Monk,

intro. David Bellos (London: Harvill, 1996), 53–55. Subsequent quotations are from this edition and are given parenthetically in the text.

5. Georges Perec, *Species of Spaces and Other Pieces*, ed. and trans. John Sturrock (London: Penguin, 2008), 13–14, original ellipsis. Subsequent quotations are from this edition and are given parenthetically in the text.

6. David Bellos, *Georges Perec: A Life in Words* (London: Harvill, 1993), 543.

7. Roland Barthes, *Roland Barthes by Roland Barthes*, trans. Richard Howard (Berkeley and Los Angeles: University of California Press, 1994). Subsequent quotations are from this edition and are given parenthetically in the text.

8. The phrase in the French original—"Ayant débité la matière de ces fragments pendant des mois"—harks back to the section title "La seiche et son encre" (the cuttlefish and its ink); Roland Barthes, *Roland Barthes par Roland Barthes* (Quercy, France: Seuil, 1975), 166.

9. Theodor Adorno, *Minima Moralia: Reflections from Damaged Life*, trans. E. F. N. Jephcott (1951; reprint, London: Verso, 1978), 36.

10. Wayne Koestenbaum, *Jackie Under My Skin: Interpreting an Icon* (1995; reprint, New York: Penguin, 1996), 90. Subsequent quotations are from this edition and are given parenthetically in the text.

11. Wayne Koestenbaum, "My '80s," originally published in *Artforum*, reprinted in *The Best American Essays 2004*, ed. Louis Menand (Boston: Houghton Mifflin Company, 2004), 128–37; and Luc Sante, "Commerce," in *New York Calling: From Blackout to Bloomberg*, ed. Marshall Berman and Brian Berger (Chicago: Reaktion Books, 2007), 102–13.

12. Carl Wilson, "My So-Called Adulthood," *New York Times Magazine*, August 4, 2011, http://www.nytimes.com/2011/08/07/magazine/the-gen-x-nostalgia-boom.html.

8. DETAILS THAT LINGER AND THE CHARM OF VOLUNTARY READING: GEORGE PELECANOS, STEPHEN KING, THOMAS PYNCHON

1. Julia Glass, *Three Junes* (2002; New York: Random House/Anchor, 2003), 192.

2. George Pelecanos, *Hard Revolution* (New York: Little, Brown, 2004), 40.

3. Stephen King, *Needful Things* (1991; reprint, New York: Penguin/Signet, 1992), 174.

4. Tim Parks, "Your English Is Showing," *New York Review Blog*, June 15, 2011, http://www.nybooks.com/blogs/nyrblog/2011/jun/15/english-showing/.

5. "For Me, England Is a Mythical Place," Tim Adams interviews Kazuo Ishiguro, *Observer*, February 20, 2005, http://www.guardian.co.uk /books/2005/feb/20/fiction.kazuoishiguro.
6. Thomas Pynchon, *Gravity's Rainbow* (1973; reprint, New York: Penguin, 2006), 81.
7. Daniel Mendelsohn, included in Juliet Lapidos, "Overrated: Authors, Critics, and Editors on 'Great Books' That Aren't All That Great," *Slate*, August 11, 2011, http://www.slate.com/id/2301312/.

9. THE IDEAL BOOKSHELF: *THE RINGS OF SATURN* AND *THE LINE OF BEAUTY*

1. W. G. Sebald, *The Rings of Saturn*, trans. Michael Hulse (New York: New Directions, 1999), first published in German in 1995 and in English translation in 1998; and Alan Hollinghurst, *The Line of Beauty* (2004; reprint, New York: Bloomsbury, 2005). Subsequent references are to these editions and will be given parenthetically in the text.
2. See Robert J. Griffin, *Wordsworth's Pope: A Study in Literary Historiography* (Cambridge: Cambridge University Press, 1995).

10. THE BIND OF LITERATURE AND THE BIND OF LIFE: *VOICES FROM CHERNOBYL*, THOMAS BERNHARD, KARL OVE KNAUSGAARD

1. Marina Van Zuylen, *Monomania: The Flight from Everyday Life in Literature and Art* (Ithaca, NY: Cornell University Press, 2005), 45, 48, 58.
2. Georges Perec, *A Man Asleep*, trans. Andrew Leak, in *Things: A Story of the Sixties and A Man Asleep* (Boston: David R. Godine, 1990), 154–55.
3. Svetlana Alexievich, *Voices from Chernobyl: The Oral History of a Nuclear Disaster*, trans. Keith Gessen (New York: Picador, 2005), 235–36.
4. Jonathan Lethem, "The Beards," in *The Disappointment Artist* (2005; reprint, New York: Vintage, 2006), 101; the subsequent passage I quote is on 142.
5. Thomas Bernhard, *Wittgenstein's Nephew: A Friendship*, trans. David McLintock, originally published in 1982 in German and first appearing in English translation in 1988 (New York: Vintage, 2009), 71. Subsequent references are to this edition and are given parenthetically in the text.
6. Karl Ove Knausgaard, *My Struggle: Book One*, trans. Don Bartlett (2009; Brooklyn, NY: Archipelago Books, 2012), 323.

A READING LIST

Alexievich, Svetlana. *Voices from Chernobyl: The Oral History of a Nuclear Disaster*. Trans. Keith Gessen. New York: Picador, 2005.

Austen, Jane. *Emma*. Ed. James Kinsley, intro. Adela Pinch. Oxford: Oxford University Press, 2003.

Barthes, Roland. *Roland Barthes by Roland Barthes*. Trans. Richard Howard. Berkeley: University of California Press, 1994.

Bellos, David. *Georges Perec: A Life in Words*. London: Harvill, 1993.

Bernhard, Thomas. *Wittgenstein's Nephew: A Friendship*. Trans. David McLintock. New York: Vintage, 2009.

Biswell, Andrew. *The Real Life of Anthony Burgess*. London: Picador, 2005.

Blake, William. *The Marriage of Heaven and Hell*. In *Complete Poetry and Prose of William Blake*, ed. David V. Erdman. Garden City, NY: Anchor Books, 1982.

Burgess, Anthony. *99 Novels: The Best in English Since 1939; A Personal Choice*. London: Allison and Busby, 1984.

Burke, Edmund. *Reflections on the Revolution in France*. Ed. Conor Cruise O'Brien. Baltimore: Penguin, 1969.

Davis, Lydia. *The Collected Stories of Lydia Davis*. New York: Farrar, Straus & Giroux, 2009.

DeWitt, Helen. *The Last Samurai*. New York: Talk Miramax, 2000.

Dickens, Charles. *David Copperfield*. Ed. Andrew Sanders. New York: Oxford University Press, 2008.

Eliot, George. *Middlemarch*. Ed. Rosemary Ashton. 1871–1872. Reprint, London: Penguin, 1994.

Fielding, Henry. *The History of Tom Jones, a Foundling.* Ed. Alice Wakely, intro. Tom Keymer. London: Penguin, 2005.

Flaherty, Alice. *The Midnight Disease: The Drive to Write, Writer's Block, and the Creative Brain.* Boston: Houghton Mifflin, 2004.

Flaubert, Gustave. *Madame Bovary: Provincial Ways.* Trans. Lydia Davis. New York: Viking Penguin, 2010.

Gaiman, Neil. *Anansi Boys.* New York: William Morrow/HarperCollins, 2005.

Himes, Chester. *Cotton Comes to Harlem.* New York: Vintage, 1988.

Hollinghurst, Alan. *The Line of Beauty.* 2004. Reprint, New York: Bloomsbury, 2005.

Jakobson, Roman. "Two Aspects of Language and Two Types of Aphasic Disturbances." In *Language in Literature,* ed. Krystyna Pomorska and Stephen Rudy. Cambridge, MA: Belknap/Harvard University Press, 1987.

James, Henry. *The Golden Bowl.* Ed. Ruth Bernard Yeazell. London: Penguin, 2009.

Jones, Edward P. *All Aunt Hagar's Children.* New York: HarperCollins/Amistad, 2006.

Kafka, Franz. *The Zürau Aphorisms of Franz Kafka.* Trans. Michael Hofman and Geoffrey Brock. New York: Schocken, 2006.

Keeler, Harry Stephen. *The Riddle of the Traveling Skull.* Ed. Paul Collins. San Francisco: McSweeney's, 2005.

Kennedy, A. L. *Paradise.* 2004. New York: Random House/Vintage, 2006.

King, Stephen. *On Writing: A Memoir of the Craft.* New York: Scribner, 2000.

Knausgaard, Karl Ove. *My Struggle: Book One.* Trans. Don Bartlett. 2009. Reprint, Brooklyn, NY: Archipelago Books, 2012.

Koestenbaum, Wayne. *Jackie Under My Skin: Interpreting an Icon.* 1995. Reprint, New York: Penguin, 1996.

——. "My '80s." In *The Best American Essays 2004,* ed. Louis Menand. Boston: Houghton Mifflin Company, 2004.

Lethem, Jonathan. "The Beards." In *The Disappointment Artist.* 2005. Reprint, New York: Vintage, 2006.

——. *The Fortress of Solitude.* 2003. Reprint, New York: Vintage, 2004.

Levi, Primo. *The Periodic Table.* Trans. Raymond Rosenthal. New York: Schocken, 1984.

Lutz, Gary. "The Sentence Is a Lonely Place." *Believer,* January 2009, http://www.believermag.com/issues/200901/?read=article_lutz.

——. *Stories in the Worst Way.* 1996. Reprint, Providence, RI: 3rd bed, 2006.

Markson, David. *Reader's Block*. Normal, IL: Dalkey Archive Press, 1996.

Nabokov, Vladimir. *Lolita*. 1955. Reprint, New York: Knopf, 1992.

Naipaul, V. S. *The Enigma of Arrival*. New York: Knopf, 1987.

——. *A House for Mr. Biswas*. 1961. Reprint, New York: Vintage, 2001.

Nell, Victor. *Lost in a Book: The Psychology of Reading for Pleasure*. New Haven, CT: Yale University Press, 1988.

Perec, Georges. *Species of Spaces and Other Pieces*. Ed. and trans. John Sturrock. London: Penguin, 2008.

Proust, Marcel. *Swann's Way*. Trans. Lydia Davis. New York: Penguin, 2004.

Pynchon, Thomas. *Gravity's Rainbow*. 1973. Reprint, New York: Penguin, 2006.

Richardson, Samuel. *Clarissa, or the History of a Young Lady*. Ed. Angus Ross. London: Penguin, 1986.

Sante, Luc. "Commerce." In *New York Calling: From Blackout to Bloomberg*, ed. Marshall Berman and Brian Berger. Chicago: Reaktion Books, 2007.

——. "French Without Tears." *Threepenny Review*, Summer 2004, http://www.threepennyreview.com/samples/sante_su04.html.

Sartre, Jean-Paul. *The Words*. Trans. Bernard Frechtman. New York: Vintage, 1981.

Sebald, W. G. *The Rings of Saturn*. Trans. Michael Hulse. New York: New Directions, 1999.

Sontag, Susan. *Against Interpretation and Other Essays*. New York: Farrar, Straus & Giroux, 1967.

Spufford, Francis. *The Child That Books Built: A Life in Reading*. New York: Metropolitan, 2002.

St. Aubyn, Edward. *The Patrick Melrose Novels*. New York: Picador, 2012.

Sterne, Laurence. *The Life and Opinions of Tristram Shandy, Gentleman*. Ed. Melvyn New and Joan New, intro. Christopher Ricks. New York: Penguin, 2003.

Temple, Peter. *The Broken Shore*. 2005. Reprint, New York: Picador, 2008.

Wolf, Maryanne. *Proust and the Squid: The Story and Science of the Reading Brain*. New York: Harper, 2007.

Wood, James. *How Fiction Works*. New York: Farrar, Straus & Giroux, 2008.

INDEX